Relationships as a *Spiritual Journey*

From Specialness to Holiness

by Robert Perry

Book #18 in a Series of Commentaries on
A Course in Miracles®

THE CIRCLE OF ATONEMENT

This is the eighteenth book in a series, each of which deals with a particular theme from the modern spiritual teaching, *A Course in Miracles* ®. The books assume a familiarity with the Course, although they might be of benefit even if you have no acquaintance with the Course. If you would like a complete listing of these books and our other publications, a sample copy of our newsletter, or information about The Circle of Atonement, please contact us at the address below.

The Circle of Atonement
Teaching and Healing Center
P.O. Box 4238, West Sedona, AZ 86340
(928) 282-0790, Fax (928) 282-0523
E-mail: info@circleofa.com
Website: www.circleofa.com

The ideas presented herein are the personal interpretation and understanding of the author, and are not necessarily endorsed by the copyright holder of *A Course in Miracles*: Foundation for *A Course in Miracles*, 41397 Buecking Dr., Temecula, CA 92590. Portions from *A Course in Miracles*, © 1996, *Psychotherapy: Purpose, Process and Practice*, and *Song of Prayer*, © 1996, reprinted by permission of the copyright holder.

All references are given for the Second Edition of the Course, and are listed according to the numbering in the Course, rather than according to page numbers. Each reference begins with a letter, which denotes the particular volume or section of the Course and its extensions (T=Text, W=Workbook for Students, M=Manual for Teachers, C=Clarification of Terms, P=Psychotherapy, and S=Song of Prayer). After this letter comes a series of numbers, which differ from volume to volume:

T, P, or S-chapter.section.paragraph:sentence; e.g., T-24.VI.2:3-4.

W-part (I or II).lesson.paragraph:sentence; e.g., W-pI.182.4:1-2.

M or C-section.paragraph:sentence; e.g., C-2.5:2.

Cover by Kathy Simes
Layout & design by Mike Jung

Published by The Circle of Atonement: Teaching and Healing Center
Printed in the United States of America

Table of Contents

Preface

Human relationships and the quest for God have traditionally not gone very well together. Our relationships are such bastions of the ego that they do not seem to really belong in the search for total enlightenment. Therefore, not only do our images of the spiritual quest often depict the aspirant trudging up the mountain by himself, but also our spiritual heroes seem to be somewhat solitary figures. Even when they are surrounded by disciples and followers they often appear to be alone, in their own world. We see them as spiritual heroes by virtue of their contact with another world, not by virtue of having whole, healthy and intimate relationships in *this* world.

A *Course in Miracles* is a departure from these traditional images, for it makes human relationships part of the spiritual quest, even central to it. In the Course's teaching we quite literally awaken to God through our relationships. They are meant to be, our salvation, not our doom (T-20.VI.11:9), and they can be our salvation *if* we are willing to completely restructure our definition of what they are for. As we do so, we discover that the journey home is not a solitary one, but that we awaken *with* our brothers. And those relationships in which we make this journey together are truly the source of our salvation (T-20.VIII.6:9).

As every Course student knows, the Course's discussion of relationships is divided into *special relationships*, which reinforce the ego, and *holy relationships*, which embody salvation. Both of these terms come from the Course and represent its unique philosophy of human relationships.

However, what that philosophy is and what those terms actually mean are issues of considerable confusion and disagreement among Course students. In the twenty years since the Course's publication, many ideas on special and holy relationships have arisen and been passed on that are not necessarily grounded in the Course itself. Indeed, many of the oldest and most widespread axioms in this area do not, in my opinion, reflect the Course. These axioms include, "there are two types of special relationships: special love and special hate," "every relationship begins as special," and, "it takes only one to make a relationship holy."

Preface

The primary purpose of this book is simply to define the terms "special relationships" and "holy relationships" and present the philosophy concerning them. Before we can transform these relationships it helps to be clear on what the Course is teaching about them. In fact, such teaching provides the foundation for the transformation. As such, this book is more of a "text" than a "workbook." It does contain some exercises in practical application; however, its main thrust is in presenting the overall framework of the Course's philosophy on special and holy relationships.

This book is a revised and combined version of two booklets which I wrote as #2 and #5 in this series (in which this book is #18). They were entitled, *Special Relationships: Illusions of Love*, and *Holy Relationships: The End of an Ancient Journey*. They have been two of our most popular booklets, and it now seemed appropriate to us to combine them and update them. I wrote these booklets based on close studies of the material in the Course which discusses special and holy relationships. Writing them provided a foundation on which my understandings could grow over the years, and this has occurred. Further, some of my understandings have not only deepened, but changed. I see now that I fell prey to some of the inaccurate lore that has grown up, and manufactured some of my own as well. For example, whereas my original booklet on special relationships reflected the common understanding that special relationships come in two classes—special love and special hate—I now believe that this schema has no foundation in the Course itself (see my discussion at the end of Chapter 1 of Part I).

Therefore, in this book the two original booklets have been revised, expanded and (in some places) corrected. This has meant expanding several of the chapters and adding two chapters to the discussion of holy relationships—a chapter on why it takes two to make a holy relationship, and one that includes an extended forgiveness process. However, in the midst of these changes I have kept the basic structure of the original booklets intact, which is why the book is divided into Part I, on special relationships, and Part II, on holy relationships.

Part One

Special
Relationships

Introduction
to Part One

*L*ove seems to be a rare and hard won thing on this earth. In our search for love our relationships with other humans are what seem to hold the greatest promise of finding it. In our relationships, especially our romantic relationship, we hope to find the love, completion, understanding, safety and warmth that we seek. *A Course in Miracles* also highly values relationships. For God is also a difficult thing to find in this world. And, according to the Course, we can most effectively find Him in our human interaction. So both the Course and the world value relationships as the means to the most prized of goals, the finding of love, or God, which the Course says are one and the same.

Yet here the similarity ends, for the Course teaches that to find God through our relationships we must utterly relinquish our current mode of relating: "...let go your imagined needs, which would destroy the relationship" (T-15.V.5:7). According to the Course, we only appear to be seeking love in our relationships. Unbeknownst to us, bubbling up from the depths of our unconscious and driving our interactions, is another need entirely. This need is guiding us in our search for love, and it is this need that we ultimately meet.

What is this need? It is quite simply the need to survive, not physically, but mentally and emotionally, to confirm our existence, to stabilize our shaky and ephemeral sense of identity. The problem, however—the core problem of human existence—is that the identity we think we have is a fundamental and comprehensive attack on the identity we really have. And so to confirm and reinforce this "identity" is to attack ourselves. This is true especially considering the fact that the glue that seems to best hold this identity together is guilt. This explains why our relationships do not work. This is why we seek love but find pain; it is pain we were seeking all along.

A Course in Miracles calls these relationships *special relationships*.

Part I of this book will be a brief examination of this topic of special relationships, one of the most important topics in the Course and in our lives. This will be my interpretation of the Course's teaching on this subtle and complex topic, an interpretation that has changed over time and still continues to evolve.

The Course's discussion of special relationships is perhaps the most dark and challenging material in the entire Course. If you can survive this, you can probably handle anything the Course has to tell you. Not that this is really any different than what the Course tells us in other places about the ego. Yet this material hits closer to home, for it takes the Course's dark vision of the ego and applies it to what we regard as our havens of love and happiness. At one point we are told, "You recognize, at least in general terms, that the ego is insane. Yet the special relationship still seems to you somehow to be 'different'" (T-17.IV.6:2-3). What this comes down to is that Part I of this book is going to be pretty dark. I will do what I can to weave in the light, just as the Course does. But still the portrait will remain very challenging.

Must this be so? Yes, says the Course. It is not only helpful, it is crucial. Many times during its admittedly difficult discussion of special relationships it pauses to remind us how important this naked facing of ego is:

> In the name of [the Son of God's] release, and in the Name of Him Who would release him, let us look more closely at the relationships the ego contrives, and let the Holy Spirit judge them truly. For it is certain that if you will look at them, you will offer them gladly to Him. What He can make of them you do not know, but you will become willing to find out, if you are willing first to perceive what you have made of them (T-15.VII.5:3-5).

So let us muster up all the determination we have to look at our egos, seeking to understand the ideas presented, but also trying to make them personal; asking ourselves how we are displaying the patterns discussed. It is essential that we not beat ourselves up for them, but simply observe them and note, calmly, humorously, how crazy our minds can be. And thus we can loosen our grip on these patterns and let them "quietly go down to dust" (W-pII.2.3:3).

Let us, therefore, be willing to look courageously at our ego's darkest and most devious manifestations, realizing that salvation, enlightenment, and even God Himself lay just the other side of them.

Little child, you are hiding your head under the cover of the heavy blankets you have laid upon yourself. You are hiding your nightmares in the darkness of your own false certainty, and refusing to open your eyes and look at them....Take off the covers and look at what you are afraid of. Only the anticipation will frighten you, for the reality of nothingness cannot be frightening....If you will look, the Holy Spirit will judge truly. Yet He cannot shine away what you keep hidden, for you have not offered it to Him and He cannot take it from you (T-12.II.4:6-7, 5:2-3, 9:7-8).

~1~

The Pursuit of Specialness and False Innocence

W hat is a special relationship? To answer that question, we must first define the word "special." "Special" means first of all, *specific*, particular, unique; one particular thing as opposed to another thing or to everything. In this sense, "special" means "set apart." Yet it also usually means more than that. It means specific in a *"good"* way: exceptional, better, superior, set above. Thus, to be special is to be both *set apart* and *set above*.

This gives us a basis for understanding what a special relationship is. It is a relationship based on specialness. Instead of seeking to love and unite with everyone, I seek to enhance my own separate identity through an exclusive interaction with one particular person. Let us break this down. A special relationship is one in which:

- I try to have a special or exclusive interaction
- with a special person
- so that I can feel more special.

To help us get in touch with the characteristics of the special relationship, the following is a list of basic assumptions that grow out of these three points. As we shall see over the course of this book, the Course claims that every one of these assumptions is totally in error.

Sacred tenets of the special relationship

- Being treated specially and made to feel special is a good thing.

- Having a special partner is a good thing.
- Other people can make me happy.
- Some people can give me more than others.
- It matters what people think of me.
- It matters how people treat me.
- I can be treated unfairly.
- Making sure I am not mistreated is a very important skill.
- It is right and good for me to point out the errors in how people treat me and tell them how to correct those errors.
- Other people make me feel things.
- Other people can attack and injure me and they have.
- Because of the bad things they have done, other people deserve my anger.
- I am honestly angry at the bad things they did.
- My anger at them is not really displaced anger at myself for my own "sins."
- My actions are caused by what other people do to me.
- I never attack first.
- People have certain roles they are supposed to fulfill in relation to my needs and my happiness.
- If they fail in these roles I have to feel bad about them.
- My picture of them is wisely informed by all of their past failures in fulfilling their role.
- In reacting to their present actions it is valid for me to respond to the entire constellation of their past actions that resemble the present action in any way.
- People owe me because of how much I have given them.
- Giving to another means loss, sacrifice, and needs to be done very cautiously.
- The way I was treated in the past continues to be relevant in the present.
- My past should have treated me better and I can prove it by my achievements in the present.
- I know who my partner is, maybe not perfectly, but roughly.
- My partner's personality matters.

- My partner's material circumstance and place in society matters.
- My partner's body—its sex, shape, weight, age, clothing, etc.—matters.
- If someone can meet my needs I should be with them, if they cannot or will not I should leave.
- Knowing how to get people to love me—through giving gifts, having an attractive personality, body and life situation, and appropriately guilting them—is a crucial skill in life.
- My attraction to certain individuals holds the promise of my future happiness.
- My attraction to them is a gift that should make them feel good about themselves. It is not an attack.
- Conflicts are best resolved by a good memory of the conflict's exact history, good bargaining skills and a willingness to compromise.

All of the above, says the Course, is intensely unnatural for us. We are vast beings, at one with all that is. To limit the scope of our love to just a few people and demand that they meet our needs is to constrict our identity and imprison ourselves. Yet in this world, special relationships seem not only natural, they seem to be the only option. How could this situation have come about? To answer that and lay a foundation for understanding what really motivates the special relationship, we must first examine the core needs that we are seeking to satisfy.

Your needs

You are a spiritual being in the Mind of God, merely dreaming that you are here in time and space. Because of this, your needs are heavenly. You need the things of God: peace, joy, happiness, wholeness, holiness. All of these are merely different aspects of love. Yet real love is God's Love; it exists only in Heaven. It is too "big"—too total, absolute, constant, impartial and immense—to "fit" in this fragmented world. This Love is also unified, indivisible. Yet when we dream that we have left Heaven, love seems to get scaled down and divided up into different aspects. The following are some of the aspects of love that we seek in our relationships.

Worth. The idea of worth is the idea that we are significant in the scheme of things, that we matter, that we are good and valuable, that we are lovable. A sense of worth is a fundamental need. Only if we feel that we have worth will we feel we have the right to experience love.

Innocence. The need to feel pure, unstained, holy, is also a fundamental need. This is evident when you observe how even the most apparently "evil" people constantly try to establish their innocence in their own eyes and in the eyes of others. We all sense that only innocence deserves love, while guilt deserves pain and punishment.

Joining. Part of love is completeness. And we only feel whole and complete when we are not alone, when we are part of a larger fabric of things. And so we join with others to feel the completion of being more than just the limited, self-bound creatures we seem to be.

The ego's needs

The above are needs we seek to satisfy in our relationships. Yet these are not by any stretch the only needs we seek to fulfill. More weighty than these needs are the ego's needs. What is the ego? The ego is nothing more than a belief within our minds. Yet it is a belief that is so ancient, rehearsed and habitual, so firmly rooted in unknown depths of consciousness, that it dominates our entire experience of reality and has dreamt into place our lives, our bodies, and the very framework of time and space in which we seem to find ourselves.

The ego is essentially the belief that I am an individual being, separate from everything that exists and cut off from the light, life and holiness of my Creator. The ego, then, is a self-concept; in fact, the foundation for all self-concepts. It is what we believe we are.

The problem, though, as I mentioned in the Introduction to Part I, is that the ego is emphatically *not* what we are. It is an *incorrect* concept of ourselves. Worse yet, it is a concept which is a direct attack on who we really are, which is to say that it is a concept that directly opposes or contradicts our true nature. To say that we are a separate, limited being that is cut off from God is an attack on the unspeakable grandeur that we really are. Therefore, to be a Son of God that believes he is an ego is to be in existential pain.

What are the ego's needs? The ego has one need and one need only: to stay in business. The way this need comes about is quite simple. While you think you are this belief we call the ego, you will associate your own survival with its survival. The idea of loosening your hold on it, or, worse yet, letting go of it entirely, is equated in your mind with loosening your hold on life itself, with teetering on the brink of the void. Your mind, therefore, over millions of years, has learned to habitually scramble to keep the ego's equilibrium, to keep it intact, just as you have learned to habitually protect your body and keep it from harm. In order to stay intact the ego directs you to constantly seek out certain things:

Separateness/lack. As we said, the bedrock of the ego is separation, the idea that I am a separate being. An inherent aspect of this is the idea that I am deeply lacking inside, for, being separate, I am cut off from reality, from the light and life of God. I not only seem to be a small portion of existence; even that small portion is empty inside. At any rate, since separateness is the stuff of the ego, the ego will do whatever it can to keep us separate from each other, to keep our minds private and alone, locked away from each other inside these bodies.

Attack. Separateness is inherently an attack. We can all recall instances of feeling attacked when someone kept his or her distance from us or, worse yet, left us. But it goes deeper than this, for the very fabric of reality is indissoluble unity. Separateness, therefore, is an attack on the oneness of reality and the Creator of that reality. The ego was produced and is maintained by attack, for without an attack on oneness there is no separateness and so no ego. All the ego does is attack in different forms; trying to play the victim and justify its attack, trying to look nice and disguise its attack, but all the while attacking simply because that is its way of life.

Guilt. The thing that really keeps the ego intact is guilt. Guilt could be called *ego mortar.* It is what makes your ego feel most secure in its existence. Why is this? The starting point of the ego is not guilt, it is separateness and attack. But guilt cements these into place by saying that the attack was real. Guilt, in fact, is simply the emotional experience of the belief that because your attack did real damage, you have committed a sin, and therefore you have made yourself into a bad person, a stained, corrupted thing that deserves punishment and death.

Fear. Guilt produces fear, fear of the punishment and death we now think we deserve, and fear *is* the ego. "The ego is quite literally a fearful thought" (T-5.V.3:7). Fear keeps the ego alive.

Death. What the above comes down to is an exceedingly startling fact: When we believe we are an ego we are motivated by the attraction to attack ourselves. This self-attack takes place through the following cycle. First, we feel a compulsion to stay separate and attack others, seemingly to protect ourselves, but really so that we can collect guilt. We want guilt because guilt produces fear. And fear is fear of the ego's final goal for us, the thing our guilt says we deserve: Death.

> The death penalty never leaves the ego's mind, for that is what it always reserves for you in the end. Wanting to kill you as the final expression of its feeling for you, it lets you live but to await death. It will torment you while you live, but its hatred is not satisfied until you die. For your destruction is the one end toward which it works, and the only end with which it will be satisfied (T-12.VII.13:2-6).

The ego is merely an idea, but an idea that when obeyed leads your own mind to attack and seek to destroy itself. So while we really want love, worth, innocence and joining in our relationships, this parasitic self-concept we have adopted demands separateness, attack, guilt, and fear from the very same relationships.

The ego's compromise

This is quite a dilemma. We have two totally opposed sets of needs within the same mind. What do we do? The following passage provides the beginning of an answer:

> The ego is certain that love is dangerous, and this is always its central teaching. It never puts it this way; on the contrary, everyone who believes that the ego is salvation seems to be intensely engaged in the search for love. Yet the ego, though encouraging the search for love very

actively, makes one proviso; do not find it. Its dictates, then, can be summed up simply as: "Seek and do not find." This is the one promise the ego holds out to you, and the one promise it will keep (T-12.IV.1:1-5).

The ego is like an employee who has to keep his boss happy with his performance at the same time that he is stealing the man blind. The ego must attack you. It cannot actually deliver love, for love means death for it. Yet at the same time it must give you at least the *promise* of finding love, for it must keep you happy with it. Thus, it has to come up with a compromise, one that accommodates both its needs and yours. Yet this compromise must only truly meet its needs while merely *seeming* to meet yours; for, again, truly filling your needs means no more ego.

The obvious solution here is to give you something that looks like love, but is really hate. It must have the apparent form of love while having the actual content of hate. In other words, the ego just disguises its hate and gives you the disguise to look at and derive "satisfaction" from. This blend of the ego's needs with your needs results in the "hybrid" needs of specialness and false innocence.

False innocence

The ego's need to accumulate guilt directly clashes with our innate need for innocence. So we turn to the ego for solution. It says that to get rid of our guilt we must project it onto others. What this means is that we blame others. We have condemned ourselves with guilt and now we try to transfer this to others by accusing them of being guilty.

The ultimate purpose of projection is always to get rid of guilt. Yet, characteristically, the ego attempts to get rid of guilt from its viewpoint only, for...the ego wants to retain guilt (T-13.II.1:1-2).

Projection is the perfect solution from the ego's standpoint. It makes us think that we are getting rid of our guilt and gaining innocence, while all the while something quite different is taking place. When we condemn another we are attacking them. And since attack is the source of guilt, by projecting guilt we are simply racking up more guilt, in the guise of getting rid of it.

Specialness

As we said, the ego's separateness entails inevitable feelings of lack and worthlessness. Separateness is the source of "your strange uneasiness, your sense of being disconnected, and your haunting fear of lack of meaning in yourself..." (T-22.I.1:6). Separateness, therefore, clashes with your need for worth.

Therefore, like a salesman who is aware that he must spice up the deal or lose the sale, the ego quickly adds, "True, being an isolated entity is no fun. But what about being an *extraordinary* isolated entity? What about being special?" Specialness is the ego's solution to the hole we feel in our souls. You could say that specialness is quality separateness; being separate in the "good" sense. If you have to live in a separated world, you might as well live in style. This specialness takes innumerable forms.

> Each worshipper of idols harbors hope his special deities will give him more than other men possess. It must be more. It does not really matter more of what; more beauty, more intelligence, more wealth, or even more affliction and more pain (T-29.VIII.8:6-8).

The need to feel special summarizes a huge amount of our perceived needs. It is virtually synonymous with the needs for status, fame, power, achievement, and human love, and is either part of or attaches itself to every other need that exists. Who of us actually questions the positive value of being special? Who does not think that being really special would make us really happy? After all, isn't being special the same thing as having worth and being lovable?

Yet it does not take a Rhodes scholar to realize that being *set above* is only a minor variation on being *set apart*. If you are special, you are alone. Further, specialness is also a form of attack, for it rests on placing others beneath you in an effort to be superior to them. Without attack there is no specialness. Only total equality is void of attack. Thus, being a form of separateness, specialness does not deliver any real sense of worth at all. It defeats its own *supposed* purpose. But it is a terrific guilt collector, which, of course, is its *real* purpose. Consider this for a moment: Feeling better than others does not deliver any real sense of worth at all. It only delivers loneliness and guilt. Believing this single fact would change our world and everyone in it.

Relationship with the world

The "needs" we are talking about can only be satisfied through a relationship with something outside of us. In our search for false innocence, we require an outer world that we can blame, a world that is guilty, that shoulders the "true" blame for the evil of which we have been accused. In other words, we need a place to dump our garbage. We cannot put it in our own house; we must find some other place outside of us that can be a dumping ground. In projecting guilt, then, we dump what we do not want onto the world.

In specialness, however, we steal what we *do* want *from* the world. How do we take specialness from the world? Specialness is inherently competitive, inherently adversarial. My specialness does not exist in a vacuum. I am only special in relation to someone else who is less special. I am set above *because* he is set below. This can even apply to humbly being less than others—we're better at being humble. Therefore, to be special, we must find someone to be better than; specialness is "better-ness." So we find someone who has at least some smidgeon of specialness and then best him, triumph over him.

By doing so, we have actually taken specialness from him. How? Whatever status or claim to fame he once had, now is ours. His title belt is around our waist. Sports, in fact, provides especially good examples of this whole process, for, like sports, this process is essentially competitive. If I take on and beat an opponent, whatever standing he had I now have. If he was not too special, beating him provides me with only a modicum of specialness. But if he was the champ, I land a lion's share.

One of my favorite examples of this "specialness transfer" is in the baseball movie, *The Natural*. Here a promising young pitcher has an unofficial "duel" with baseball's greatest hitter, the Whammer. A crowd of people is looking on, including a pretty young woman, who is fascinated by the Whammer's abilities and whom the Whammer has been trying to impress. When the pitcher finally strikes out the Whammer, we are shown, in slow motion, the woman's reverent gaze detach from the Whammer, move across the field, and fix itself on the young pitcher.

This draws out another aspect of acquiring specialness. To get specialness, in addition to a loser, there must be an *audience*, someone who gives us the acknowledgment of specialness, who gives us the message, with her gaze, her words, her deeds and her body, "You are special."

In summary, by being better than someone else, I prove myself to be special and actually acquire the specialness that he used to possess. The acknowledgment of specialness that the world gave him it now gives me. And having this acknowledgment, my specialness is made real. I have stolen specialness from outside myself and used it to fill the emptiness within me.

The unadorned egoic relationship

You can imagine what kind of relationships would be produced by these two drives: the need to steal specialness from the world and the need to dump our guilt on the world. Unless these drives were disguised, tempered and suppressed, they would produce relationships of pure hatred and hostility. And we do see these relationships in the world, between people who are called enemies. I think it is safe to say that such relationships are the minority of our relationships—for most of us, the very small minority. Yet they provide an instructive glimpse into the more undisguised dynamics of the ego. They are like a modern caveman, a living remnant of a more primitive form of ego functioning.

Let us look at the core activity of such relationships. This activity is exceedingly important, for, while following the ego, it is *all we ever do*. It is the ego's single activity. This activity weaves together both of the processes just outlined, projecting guilt to gain false innocence, and attacking to gain specialness. This single, all-encompassing dynamic is given its best description in the section entitled, "The Laws of Chaos" (T-23.II), which provides much of the basis for the following discussion.

The process begins in the beginning, with us separating, throwing God away, as the Course says. This leaves us feeling empty, alone and guilty. The guilt is unbearable. How can we get free of it? We blame our condition on our brothers. They took God away from us.

> ...by projecting your own rejection you believe that others are taking it from you. You must be fearful if you believe that your brother is attacking you to tear the Kingdom of Heaven from you. This is the ultimate basis for all the ego's projection (T-7.VII.8:3-5).

In other words, we are not responsible for losing God, we are not responsible for our current unhappy state; our brother is. He stole God from us. He made us unhappy. He provoked our attack. This projection of blame seems to bring relief, for we feel tremendous guilt for throwing God away. By blaming our brother, this guilt appears to be relieved. One goal, that of false innocence, has already been achieved.

Yet this is not enough; we want what our brother "stole" returned to us. A slight twist enters, here, however: We threw God away because we thought we did not want Him. So now we are looking not for God, but for a *substitute* for God, a pseudo-Heaven, an artificial love. This is specialness. So in our twisted minds we accuse our brother of stealing our specialness and keeping it for himself.

> And now you understand the reason why you found it not. For it was taken from you by this enemy, and hidden where you would not think to look. He hid it in his body, making it the cover for his guilt, the hiding place for what belongs to you....This is the magic that will cure all of your pain; the missing factor in your madness that makes it "sane." This is the reason why you must attack. Here is what makes your vengeance justified. Behold, unveiled, the ego's secret gift, torn from your brother's body, hidden there in malice and in hatred for the one to whom the gift belongs. He would deprive you of the secret ingredient that would give meaning to your life. The substitute for love...must be salvation....And all your relationships have but the purpose of seizing it and making it your own (T-23.II.11:4-6, 12:5-12).

Claiming that our treasure was stolen by our brother is a deft move psychologically. For not only does it yield a sense of false innocence, it says that what our brother has is really *ours*. He does not deserve to have it, he should give it back. And if he does not, we are perfectly justified in taking it from him and punishing him in the process. Our attack on him becomes necessary, righteous, *innocent*. We do not want to attack (or so we say), "But in a savage world the kind cannot survive, so they must take or else be taken from" (T-23.II.10:4). If, then, we are successful in recovering our treasure of specialness, we emerge with both objectives met: We are both special and guiltless.

The process could be summarized thusly: "You are guilty of the loss of my specialness and I am justified in stealing it back. You deserve my guilt and I deserve your specialness." This single process has a certain brilliance to it, you must admit. In one fell swoop it acquires for me both false innocence and specialness, and in such a way that the false innocence makes way for the acquisition of specialness. By accusing you of theft, I dump my guilt over separating from God onto you. This justifies me in stealing from you a substitute for God: specialness. And any guilt that I would acquire from stealing this I then dump back on you, saying you forced my attack.

I realize this sounds very abstract, for we are not entirely conscious of these dynamics. We do not go around thinking, "You are responsible for my separation from God." However, think about when you are angry with someone. Isn't it *always* because they supposedly took something from you—your self-esteem, your peace, your happiness? And because they took it, two things now result. First, they are guilty while you are innocent (which, let's admit it, feels good). And second, they deserve to pay, to pay you back for what they took, to restore your property, with interest. And if they don't pay, you are completely within your rights, and completely innocent, in extracting payment from them.

We could go into these dynamics even further. The very fact that they are the guilty one makes them less special and makes you more special, an "unexpected" pleasure in a trying situation. The very fact that you make them pay is an act of triumph that further elevates you above them, thus enhancing your specialness. Finally, your specialness makes it quite natural for you to judge and blame them, since you are their superior, looking down upon them from above. Specialness and innocence thus go hand in hand, each feeding the other. It is an ugly scenario. Yet if we are really honest with ourselves, do we not find ourselves immersed in this scenario many times each day?

From the ego's standpoint this process seems perfect, though *not* because it really delivers worth (the supposed pay-off of specialness) and innocence, but because it delivers lack and guilt. What has actually happened is that the ego has tricked us into attacking, both through blaming and through competing. Thus it has tricked us into affirming over and over that we are guilty (though we may not always be conscious of this feeling).

Further, it has fooled us into looking for our worth outside ourselves. Thus, each ounce of energy we placed into this search was an affirmation that completion is there outside of us. And so that is what we end up believing: that completion is outside and lack is within. This pursuit of specialness and false innocence, then, does not fill our needs at all, but it is extremely effective in filling the *ego's* needs.

A note on "special hate"

What I am calling here the unadorned egoic relationship is what is commonly called by Course students "the special hate relationship." In fact, I myself called it that in the booklet that this book is a revision of. Almost all of us learned early on in our journey with the Course that there are *two* types of special relationship: special hate and special love. I now believe, though, that we did not learn this from the *Course*. We inherited it through what I call Course lore, a body of ideas that have been handed down about the Course which may not accurately reflect the Course.

I say that based on two crucial facts. First, what we call the special hate relationship is called that in the Course only *once*. The term "special hate relationship" occurs a single time: "Be not afraid to look upon the special hate relationship, for freedom lies in looking at it" (T-16.IV.1:1). Rather than being part of the Course's vocabulary, the term is actually an anomaly, something that crops up once and does not fit the general pattern of the Course's terminology.

Second, when the term "special relationship" is used in the Course, as it is dozens of times, it does not refer to an overall class that includes within it two smaller classes called "special hate" and "special love." Instead, "special relationship" is a *synonym*, pure and simple, for "special love relationship." They are two (very slightly) different terms for the same thing. To really demonstrate this I would have to walk you through 75 references to special relationships, which there is not space here to do. Yet you can look through the references yourself if you have the *Concordance of A Course in Miracles*. If you do, I believe you will see that the Course says the exact same things about special relationships as it does about special *love* relationships. Both are spoken of as a relationship that we are attracted to and think is happy and loving, yet which beneath the outer veneer is full of hate, guilt and fear. This is the point of all the Course's special relationship discussions—to take the loving disguise off of our friendships and romances.

This, by the way, is also true of the term "unholy relationship." It, too, is a synonym for "special love relationship" (even though it is listed in the *Concordance* under "special hate").

In short, "special relationship," "special love relationship," and "unholy relationship," are all the same thing. They are all *special love*. This is important to point out, for otherwise when we read "special relationship" in the Course we will think, "This means both special love and special hate." This waters down the point of taking the disguise off of special love. Worse yet, when we read "unholy relationship" we will think, "This means special hate," when actually it is talking about special love. For all of the above reasons, then, I propose that we drop the term "special hate relationship" from our Course vocabulary.

~2~
The Special Love Relationship: The Great Narrowing

As you may guess after reading the preceding chapter, the unadorned pursuit of specialness and false innocence (which we can simply call "hate" rather than "special hate") would be extremely unsatisfying as a total way of life. Imagine if literally everyone was your enemy, the focus of your blame, a mere stepping-stone for your climb up the ladder of specialness. What a bleak life! For this reason, even the most apparently evil people in the world almost always surround themselves with "loyal" and "trusted" friends and loved ones.

The reason is obvious. Having nothing but enemies meets none of your needs very well at all. Earlier we mentioned three needs that you have, three aspects of love: worth, innocence and joining. Let us look one by one at how well these are met by hate. In hate you are looking to others to make you feel special, to give you a sense of worth. Yet hated enemies, at best, give only grudging acknowledgment of specialness. You have to wring it out of them. And even then it is not wholehearted. Further, you do not feel all that innocent when you are in the midst of hate. And most of all, your need for joining is completely unmet by hate. You are alone. I recall hearing that near the end of his life, Orson Welles said that he would rather be looked upon as a nice guy than a difficult genius. Most of us would trade a little companionship for a lot of specialness.

In other words, hate—the raw act of dumping guilt and grabbing specialness—is too pure an expression of the ego. Its needs are met extremely well, but are too obviously met at the expense of yours. With only this modality, the ego would be judged unsatisfying and would be "fired." To defend its very "life," then, the ego needs to come up with something else, a better illusion, one that still meets its own needs while also *seeming* to meet yours. And, as may be expected, the ego rises to the occasion. Out of the pressures of this challenge, the ego comes up with its greatest achievement, its "most boasted gift" (T-16.V.3:1): the special love relationship. In it, the ego achieves the apparent perfect mix of what it wants and what you want.

> The special relationship is a strange and unnatural ego device for joining hell and Heaven, and making them indistinguishable. And the attempt to find the imagined "best" of both worlds has merely led to fantasies of both, and to the inability to perceive either as it is. The special relationship is the triumph of this confusion. It is a kind of union from which union is excluded, and the basis for the attempt at union rests on exclusion. What better example could there be of the ego's maxim, "Seek but do not find?" (T-16.V.6)

The special relationship is based on your desire to find love yet also hang onto hate. This desire seems quite natural in this world. "No one considers it bizarre to love and hate together, and even those who believe that hate is sin merely feel guilty, but do not correct it" (T-16.V.3:4). And so we mix love and hate together and they seem to exist quite comfortably side-by-side. Our special love relationships exist right alongside our hate relationships. The people we "love" are right next to the people we reject. We even both love and hate our special love partners.

Yet hate and love cannot go together. To think they can is to misunderstand the nature of love. For, "You can love only as God loves" (T-13.X.11:4), as the following passage so eloquently states:

> There is no other love that can satisfy you, because there is no other love. This is the only love that is fully given and fully returned. Being complete, it asks nothing. Being wholly pure, everyone joined in it has everything. This is not the basis for any relationship in which the ego enters. For every relationship on which the ego embarks is special (T-15.VII.1:2-7).

According to the Course's lofty definition of love, real love only gives. It places no demands whatsoever and allows complete freedom. To love is to give all of yourself away to everyone at once, all the time, without any partiality, selectivity or variation. Rather than the ultimate sacrifice, this is the ultimate ecstasy. For like God, "you can give yourself completely, wholly without loss and only with gain" (T-15.VI.4:6).

Love, therefore, is a total idea. In love, what you give is total. You give it to totality, to everything. And the duration of your giving is total; you never let up. This totality is part of love's nature. If you pull back even a little bit on the totality of your love, if you make one exception, you lose the understanding of what love is. Thus, it goes without saying that trying to mix love with hate *completely* obscures love's meaning. In fact, it even obscures hate's meaning, for you start getting the two mixed up, confusing one with the other. You think that the hate you give your partner is actually love and you shun real love as if it were a hated thing.

What are we doing, then, in our "love" relationships? Well, I believe the Course would admit that sometimes, perhaps often, a weak reflection of real love, what you could call semi-right-minded love, squeaks through in our relationships. But this is carefully penned in. It is not the dominant force in the relationship, for if it were, the people involved would quickly become authentic saints.

We must admit that from the Course's perspective, most of what passes for love in our relationships is a pure illusion. It is really just disguised hate, hate made to look like love. It is the *apparent form* of love cloaking the *actual content* of hate. It "is nothing more than an 'attractive' form of fear, in which the guilt is buried deep and rises in the form of 'love'" (T-16.V.8:5). In the powerful section called "The Two Pictures," this apparent form of love is likened to a picture enclosed in a massive, elaborate frame, into which

> ...are woven all sorts of fanciful and fragmented illusions of love, set with dreams of sacrifice and self-aggrandizement, and interlaced with gilded threads of self-destruction. The glitter of blood shines like rubies, and the tears are faceted like diamonds and gleam in the dim light in which the offering is made (T-17.IV.8:3-4).

The seemingly attractive frame is meant to keep our eyes fixed on its "hypnotic gleaming" (T-17.IV.9:10), so that we do not realize that the actual picture it surrounds is a picture of death, the outcome of hate. This is how the ego keeps itself in business; this is how it defends itself. This is how it sweetens the deal and keeps us hanging on. By convincing us that we can find love and happiness within its system, it lulls us into thinking that we need never wake up to God. Why should we? We can find what we want right here. This explains that dramatic but puzzling statement from the Course, "The special love relationship is the ego's chief weapon for keeping you from Heaven" (T-16.V.2:3).

Special love is not real love. It is just an illusion of love. This is why our "love" is so unstable and undependable—and so fleeting. The reason we become disillusioned in our relationships is that we realize the love we thought was there was only an illusion. And we are right. "Love is not an illusion. It is a fact. Where disillusionment is possible, there was not love but hate" (T-16.IV.4:1-3).

How can this be? How can our havens of love, our refuges in a harsh world, be something so different from how they appear? The rest of Part I will attempt to answer this question, as well as provide suggestions for the way out.

Narrowing down the crowd

The special love relationship involves an incredible narrowing down of the Sonship, selecting increasingly small aspects of the totality with which to relate. This narrowing begins by seeking out particular parts of the Sonship—particular people—to meet your needs. This seems to be the most natural thing in the world. Some people are simply more suitable for you. Some are better able to meet your needs than others. This is obvious. So we spend a lifetime searching for that special someone who can love us, who can treat us right, who can give us what we deserve, who can understand what we are really about.

Yet this single idea, so seemingly obvious, is an enormous step, a daring interpretation on our part. "How can you decide that special aspects of the Sonship can give you more than others?" (T-15.V.3:5) The fact, according to the Course, is that they cannot. *No one person can satisfy us more than any other.* In Heaven we have an equally complete and total relationship with every single living thing. No relationship is any different or any more special. Even on earth we can experience a mirror of this fact:

> Under the Holy Spirit's teaching all relationships are seen
> as total commitments, yet they do not conflict with one
> another in any way. Perfect faith in each one, for its ability
> to satisfy you completely, arises only from perfect faith in
> yourself (T-15.VI.1:3-4).

Obviously, on a form level we cannot give all of our time and all that we have to everyone. In this world, relationships have to take different forms and assume different places in our lives, some large, some small. But a truly illumined perspective is to be equally and totally devoted to each person, regardless of the place that person occupies in your life.

Therefore, to "select certain ones as partners in any aspect of living, and use them for any purpose which [you] would not share with others" (T-16.IV.4:5), is to attack the oneness of reality and to feel guilty for doing so:

> We have said that to limit love to part of the Sonship is to bring guilt into your relationships, and thus make them unreal. If you seek to separate out certain aspects of the totality and look to them to meet your imagined needs, you are attempting to use separation to save you. How, then, could guilt not enter? For separation is the source of guilt, and to appeal to it for salvation is to believe you are alone. To be alone is to be guilty. For to experience yourself as alone is to deny the Oneness of the Father and His Son, and thus to attack reality (T-15.V.2:2-7).

This may seem to present us with a hopeless dilemma, for it is impossible to have a relationship with everyone while on earth. It seems that in this world we absolutely must populate our lives with a limited number of people. And the Course agrees with this: "...from a practical point of view he cannot meet everyone, nor can everyone find him. Therefore, the plan includes very specific contacts to be made for each teacher of God" (M-3.1:4-5). While in this world, we must engage in the form of specialness. The point is to fill this form of specialness with the content of holiness, to love our companion as a symbol of the entire Sonship. And that is enough. For, we are told at one point, "If one such union were made in perfect faith, the universe would enter into it" (T-16.VI.5:6).

Narrowing our partner down to a body

All right, we have chosen our companion, having narrowed her down from a very large field indeed, the field of infinity. Now what? Well, we certainly do not want all of her. Since her reality in its entirety is the entire Sonship, accepting all of her puts us right back where we started. So in the spirit of the endeavor, we must pare her down, too. "...the special relationship the ego seeks does not include even one whole individual. The ego wants but part of him, and sees only this part and nothing else" (T-16.VI.5:7-8). This part is the body.

> Yet [the two individuals] only seem to be together. For relationships, to the ego, mean only that bodies are together. It is always this that the ego demands, and it does not object where the mind goes or what it thinks, for this seems unimportant. As long as the body is there to receive its sacrifice, it is content. To the ego the mind is private, and only the body can be shared (T-15.VII.8:1-5).

It is obvious that the special relationship is heavily concerned with bodies, how thin, how fat, how young, how old, how well-dressed, how healthy, how sick, how shapely, how muscular, how the head looks—the face, the eyes, the mouth, the hair, how certain parts are—how big, small, firm, flabby, etc. We are obsessed with bodies, and even if we do not care too much how our own body looks, we usually still care how other bodies look. I remember hearing about a poll taken of college students, asking them what factors figured into their estimation of someone. I think physical appearance was rated something like fourth. Give me a break! We do not like to admit it, but someone's appearance is very close to the top of the list in importance, at times at the very top.

But isn't this a little unfair? We are not solely concerned with people's bodies per se. Saying that we are does not do justice to what actually happens in our relationships. For we do value people's inner qualities. And this is demonstrated by the fact that we often choose someone with an entertaining personality over someone who is better looking. Sometimes we even choose to spend our lives with someone who is disfigured or is an invalid.

We need to look a little more closely at what the Course is saying. In one helpful passage it clarifies that we are not solely concerned with the body for the sake of what it looks like, but also for the sake of what

> a body does....A person says something you do not like. He does something that displeases you. He "betrays" his hostile thoughts in his behavior. You are not dealing here

with what the person is. On the contrary, you are exclusively concerned with what he does in a body (W-pI.72.3:3-4:2).

In light of this passage, this, I believe, is what the Course is saying: We *do* value people for more than just their bodies. We do value their inner qualities, but in our usual, ego-based thinking, these inner qualities have scarce little importance *on their own*. For we consider reality to be the physical realm. Only what occurs in that "reality" is seen to be real. The mental realm is considered private and therefore only takes on reality in our eyes as it is expressed in the physical realm. Therefore, only as a person's inner qualities are expressed through their *behavior* do those qualities seem significant. Saying that we value someone's personality is simply saying that we value what their body says and does.

Let's say I have fantasies about someone besides my wife. By themselves those fantasies do not mean very much in our usual way of thinking. It is only as those fantasies affect my behavior that they appear important; only as they cause me to physically demonstrate less love to my wife, perhaps even to cheat on her or to leave her. It is what happens in the bodily "reality" that matters. Inner realities are only important insofar as they affect that "reality." "To the ego the mind is private, and only the body can be shared. Ideas are basically of no concern, except as they bring the body of another closer or farther" (T-15.VII.8:5-6). Of course, this thinking is the opposite of the truth, which says it is the mind that is real, not the body.

What this adds up to is that in the special relationship the goal is to get a body to behave in certain ways to me. For, since bodies are ultimately real, their behavior is inherently meaningful. There is inherent meaning in a body's face smiling at me, or a body's hand touching my body, or being allowed to touch certain parts on another body. Thus, like Aladdin's lamp, bodies are seen to possess some kind of magical power that is actually able to grant me more reality. If I am surrounded by a great many bodies that are performing really special behaviors towards me, then I become ultra-special and exceptionally real.

In the special relationship, then, it is bodies that we join with. Their togetherness, the interaction of their eyes, mouths and hands, is what constitutes a relationship. And if those bodies are not able to interact, the relationship is not able to take place. What is this, asks the Course, except an excuse to keep minds separate, and therefore a defense against real joining? A body is not a mind, and so to substitute the joining of bodies for the joining of minds is to defend against true mental joining.

> ...they think their minds must be kept private or they will lose them, but if their bodies are together their minds remain their own. The union of bodies thus becomes the way in which they would keep minds apart (T-15.VII.11:5-6).

In other words, the ego is terrified of real joining, for if you truly join with another, the ego is gone. So just as the ego used one individual as a substitute for the entire Sonship, so the ego uses the body as a substitute for that individual. It teaches that the person himself is dangerous, for he represents the extinguishment of your boundaries. Therefore, it says, if you must satisfy this insane need for companionship, at least keep your mind to yourself and only allow your body to enter into the relationship. This, you could say, is the ego's prenuptial agreement.

Narrowing it down to certain body parts

Yet this narrowing process does not stop with our brother's body. It goes even further:

> No one is seen complete. The body is emphasized, with special emphasis on certain parts, and used as the standard for comparison of acceptance or rejection for acting out a special form of fear (T-18.I.3:6-7).

> For even the body of another, already a severely limited perception of him, is not the central focus as it is, or in entirety. [Certain parts are]...centered on and separated off as being the only parts of value. Every step in the making, the maintaining and the breaking off of the unholy relationship is a move toward further fragmentation and unreality (T-17.III.3:2-4).

Does this mean that I chose my mate simply because he or she had a pretty face, or big muscles, or terrific legs? Maybe you did, but these passages need not mean only that. Remember that we do value people's inner qualities, but only as they become manifest through their bodies. For instance, if you chose someone because you loved the quality of his voice, then to a significant degree he is a mouth and throat to you. And if he permanently loses his voice, then you have lost a huge part of who he is.

Whether I value body parts as ends in themselves, or as means for expressing what is inside, the point is that I regard someone as a collection of certain body parts. Clearly, our narrowing process has reached an extreme point here. This is so degrading that it sounds degrading even to us, who have already degraded ourselves almost infinitely, from an eternal Son of God to a lowly animal on planet Earth.

Substitution

The narrowing, however, does not stop there. Once we narrow someone down to a pile of special body parts, we go one more step. We narrow that pile down *in importance*, assigning it a limited place in our lives, a particular position in our hierarchy of parts-piles.

> The ego's use of relationships is so fragmented that it frequently goes even farther; one part of one aspect [of the Sonship—one person] suits its purpose, while it prefers different parts of another aspect. Thus does it assemble reality to its own capricious liking, offering for your seeking a picture whose likeness does not exist. For there is nothing in Heaven or earth that it resembles, and so, however much you seek for its reality, you cannot find it because it is not real (T-15.V.7).

In other words, we find one person's body parts unable to satisfy some need in us, and so replace it with another person's body parts that can satisfy that need. The Course calls this process "substitution."

> To substitute is to accept instead...to choose between, renouncing one aspect of the Sonship in favor of the other. For this special purpose, one is judged more valuable and the other is replaced by him....substitution is the strongest defense the ego has for separation (T-18.I.1).

The entire narrowing process that we have traced is a process of substitution. First, we substituted particular brothers for the totality of the

Sonship. Then we substituted one of these brothers for another. Then we substituted the body for the mind. Then particular bodies for other bodies. Then body parts for the whole body. Then particular collections of parts for other collections. Then parts of our relationship with one collection with other parts of our relationship with the same collection. All of this is the natural result of the original substitution that began it all:

> You who believe that God is fear made but one substitution. It has taken many forms, because it was the substitution of illusion for truth; of fragmentation for wholeness. It has become so splintered and subdivided and divided again, over and over, that it is now almost impossible to perceive it once was one, and still is what it was....Everything you see reflects it, and every special relationship that you have ever made is part of it (T-18.I.4).

The way out, therefore, is not to choose our partners better. It is to stop this process of choosing between, of separating people out from each other and pitting one person against another in our mind. The Course is telling us that there is absolutely no need to choose between people. It is possible to love them all equally in our heart, even though our relationships with them will inevitably take different forms in a world of form.

Joining with a fantasy

All in all, our effort to find companionship and joining has at the same time been based on the total fear of real joining. We fear that if we really erase our boundaries and come face to face with the reality behind the body we see, our egos will vanish and we will cease to exist as we now know ourselves. And so, rather than join with the reality of other people, we have converted them into fantasy pictures in our minds. And it is to these self-made images we relate; it is with these we "join." Thus, the Course is making the shocking claim that, although we have supposedly grown up, every relationship we have is really with an imaginary playmate:

> The "ideal" of the unholy relationship thus becomes one in which the reality of the other does not enter at all to "spoil" the dream. And the less the other really brings to

the relationship, the "better" it becomes. Thus, the attempt at union becomes a way of excluding even the one with whom the union was sought. For it was formed to get him out of it, and join with fantasies in uninterrupted "bliss" (T-17.III.4:5-8).

As a result, the most important thing we can bring to any relationship is the willingness to know the other person as he truly is, to see behind his body, behind the mask he shows to us, behind even the mask he shows to himself, to the Person he truly is in reality, the radiant Being that God knows as him. And by seeing his reality we are seeing our own. We are looking in the mirror and seeing our own true face, for in reality we are that exact same Person, that same radiant Being.

~3~
The Bargain

*U*sing our narrowing down process, the process of substitution, we now have a partner; actually, we have several partners: romantic partner(s), friends, family, perhaps children. Now the question is: What do we want from them?

We want specialness, of course. Only now we don't get it by forcibly triumphing over them. Instead, they give it to us through their "love." To describe how this works, I find it helpful to think of specialness as an actual, semi-physical energy, for that is exactly how we experience it. Someone who is special feels to us to be surrounded by an aura of importance, significance, value, desirability. We cannot see this aura—for it is purely imaginary—but we all "know" when it is there. We all know who has it and who does not.

This energy of specialness, then, is possessed by certain people. It radiates from their bodies and, what's more, can be *transmitted* by those bodies. It is transmitted through facial expressions, physical gestures, spoken words, signatures, etc., through sending the message, "You are special." This is the body's magical power that we spoke of in the last chapter. This is the genie in the lamp, a genie who is able to come out of the lamp (the body) and grant wishes.

For instance, if a really special person physically interacts with you, then some of their glow is transmitted to you. You acquire some of their specialness. I recently met a woman who once kissed Elvis Presley in a movie they were in together. And though it was probably over thirty years ago, she is still asked about it all the time. Some of the specialness that was transferred in that kiss still sparkles around her today.

So this specialness is transmitted by bodies that possess it; in particular, by certain behaviors performed by certain body parts. And again, we all know *which* behaviors and *which* body parts. Had Elvis just signed an autograph for her, that would be a different matter. Had he spent the night with her, that too would be a different matter.

This, then, is what we want from those collections of body parts we discussed in the last chapter. First we want a person who in our eyes glows like a specialness supernova. And then we want their glowing body parts to transmit their specialness glow to us, by speaking certain words to us, giving us flowers, kissing us, touching us, looking at us in a certain way, putting rings on our fingers, saying, "I do," etc.

In addition to specialness, we are looking for false innocence from these people, but not by blaming and guilting them (at least at first). Instead, we want them to *join us* in blaming all our enemies, all those people who did us wrong. We want them to stick up for us, to affirm that we were right and the other guy was wrong. We want them to do this actively and vocally, but they also do this by their mere presence. For a special love partner is a trophy, the very presence of which tells all the people from our past that they were wrong about us. For, see, here we have won the love, the credit, the belief, they refused to give us. This proves that we really did deserve it all along, just as we said, in spite of their stubborn refusal to give it to us. Our partner's gift of specialness proves that we were right in blaming all those people and asserting our innocence. Just as before, specialness and false innocence go hand-in-hand.

Yet how can we obtain these wondrous gifts from our wondrously special partner? We would, of course, prefer to just take them. But this time direct attack is not going to work. No one is going to lavish their specialness on us if we attack directly. We are going to have to give something of value to receive more value. This complicates things immensely, for according to our current way of thinking, what we give, we lose.

> To the ego, to give anything implies that you will have to do without it. When you associate giving with sacrifice, you give only because you believe that you are somehow getting something better, and can therefore do without the thing you give. "Giving to get" is an inescapable law of the ego (T-4.II.6:3-5).

It is easy to see how we lose when we give away material gifts. Yet we also feel that we lose when we give away our time, energy, attention, and our love. Therefore, to acquire the specialness we seek, we will have to make a sacrifice. We cannot just reach out and take what we want. We have to undergo loss to experience gain. As the saying goes: no pain, no gain.

We, in fact, are going to have to give away some of the very affirmation of specialness that we are seeking to obtain.

How regrettable! And what a potential waste, for unless we are careful, we might give our specialness away and not get enough back, making the whole affair a losing proposition. Many versions of this could happen. The other person may simply take our specialness and not give anything back. Or they may give too little back. Or they may seem to give as much as we do, but their specialness may actually be worth less than ours is. Or we may give more than we need to, obtaining something that we could have received for less of an outlay.

In order to protect ourselves from these unfortunate possibilities we have to make an agreement with the person, a deal, a bargain. Both of us must either consciously or unconsciously sign a contract which details what we need to give to each other in exchange for what we receive. Sometimes this is a very quick and easy process. Sometimes it requires years of effort and perhaps even formal negotiators—mediators, lawyers, counselors, etc.

The transaction

Now let us look at the actual transaction. What really happens as we exchange our specialness? This is a very important question, for our transactions can seem so pleasant and loving. Often, each person can appear to be just giving out of a heart that is overflowing with love and generosity. Or, where the bargain is overt and conscious, still both people can seem quite pleased with the terms and therefore seem to be engaging in the transaction with nothing but goodwill. But, according to the Course, there is a much deeper and more sinister reality behind bargaining. Before we can let go of the special relationship it is this we must see.

Let us trace this transaction, then, beginning with your act of "giving." As per agreement, you give your partner a certain amount of specialness. Why do you do this? What is behind your giving?

The desire to get. We have already discussed this. The sad fact is that most "giving" that takes place in this world is not real giving. It is not given simply for its own sake, but in payment for something else. You recognize that unless you give something you will get nothing back. The fact is, most of your "gifts" are made according to an unspoken agreement that labels your seeming gift as payment in a business deal.

[God's gifts] are not like to the gifts the world can give, in

which the giver loses as he gives the gift; the taker is the
richer by his loss. Such are not gifts, but bargains made
with guilt. The truly given gift entails no loss. It is
impossible that one can gain because another loses....No
gift is given thus. Such "gifts" are but a bid for a more
valuable return; a loan with interest to be paid in full; a
temporary lending, meant to be a pledge of debt to be
repaid with more than was received by him who took the
gift. This strange distortion of what giving means pervades
all levels of the world you see. It strips all meaning from
the gifts you give, and leaves you nothing in the ones you
take (W-105.1:4-2:4).

Atoning for your guilt. If someone has already given to you or if
you expect to receive something from him, you must give something in
return, or you are guilty of stealing. And so you give to allay this sense of
guilt, to erase your debt, to show that you are a good person and not a thief.

Attacking the other to instill guilt. Now we are getting to the dark
underbelly of the bargain. What is payment really all about? Why does
paying you compel you to give me something? What power does payment
exert over you? The Course seems to suggest that the power payment has is
the simple power of guilt. Let us look at this.

If I give you something that has value, I have lost that value and
you have gained it. The value has transferred from me to you, leaving me
empty and you full. You, then, are responsible for my loss. You are guilty of
my loss. Your guilt places you in debt to me. And this gives me the right to
demand payment from you, in order to heal my loss and cleanse your guilt.

For each one thinks that he has sacrificed something to the
other, and hates him for it....And for this sacrifice, which
he demands of himself, he demands that the other accept
the guilt and sacrifice himself as well (T-15.VII.7:2,6).

This has profound implications. For what this means is that
bargaining, which is really the basis of every system in our society, is guilt-
based. Contracts, deals, obligations, reciprocity, all rest on guilt. When I pay
you I do so to make you indebted to me, or to pay off my debt to you. And
what is debt? Financial debt is physical guilt. Emotional debt is emotional

guilt, i.e., just plain guilt. The same with obligation. Webster's dictionary says that obligation has to do with "the demands of conscience," with "feeling or being indebted esp. legally, ethically, or socially." In short, all payment works by the power of guilt. By paying you I place you in a position of guilt, and the only way to erase your guilt is to pay me back.

What this means is that gift-giving is usually an expression of anger. It may not seem like anger when I pay you, when I hand you my money at your yard sale, when I reciprocate or give you a gift out of obligation. But if I am engaging in a bargain, overt or covert, my payment is an attempt to instill guilt in you. And the only thing that can instill guilt is anger.

> Anger takes many forms, but it cannot long deceive those who will learn that love brings no guilt at all, and what brings guilt cannot be love and must be anger. All anger is nothing more than an attempt to make someone feel guilty, and this attempt is the only basis the ego accepts for special relationships (T-15.VII.10:2-3).

> The "sacrifice," which [the ego] regards as purification, is actually the root of its bitter resentment. For it would prefer to attack directly, and avoid delaying what it really wants. Yet the ego acknowledges "reality" as it sees it, and recognizes that no one could interpret direct attack as love. Yet to make guilty is direct attack, although it does not seem to be (T-15.VII.6:2-5).

Why am I angry at having to sacrifice to you? Why is it the root of my bitter resentment? Simply because I resent having to give up something. I would rather just take what I want. Thus, even when our bargain seems to be a fair trade, I will still be angry at having to sacrifice to you. Somewhere in my mind I will be thinking that if you were not so selfish, you would have just given it to me, and not required that I reciprocate.

~ ~ ~

Let us, therefore, summarize just what is motivating my gift to you. When I sacrifice something to you first, I am making you responsible for my loss. I am *attacking you to instill guilt* and placing a demand on you to restore my loss. When I sacrifice to you second, I am filling the loss you incurred by giving to me, and thus am *atoning for my own guilt.*

What makes both of these worthwhile is *the desire to get.* I prefer your treasure to mine. This makes me willing to sacrifice my treasure to obtain yours, either to acquire yours or to pay off what I already acquired.

The currency: our "selves"

What exactly is being exchanged in this transaction? What is the currency being traded? On the outside it appears to be various physical things, including physical behaviors, gestures of love and friendship. Yet, as we saw at the beginning of this chapter, what is really exchanged is the "energy" of specialness. That is what we are actually passing back and forth, the physical things and behaviors being simply the carriers or transmitters of that energy. In its fullest form, however, what we are exchanging is our very identities, as we conceive them. We are exchanging the sum total of our specialness, which *is* how we conceive of our identities. We are trying to give away our "self" and get back a better one.

> Each partner tries to sacrifice the self he does not want for one he thinks he would prefer. And he feels guilty for the "sin" of taking, and of giving nothing of value in return. How much value can he place upon a self that he would give away to get a "better" one?
>
> The "better" self the ego seeks is always one that is more special. And whoever seems to possess a special self is "loved" for what can be taken from him. Where both partners see this special self in each other, the ego sees a "union made in Heaven" (T-16.V.7:5-8:3).

So, in special love relationships we are trying to trade selves. We do not like the self we have (or think we have) and for a seemingly good reason: it is not special enough. "And you despise it because you do not think it offers the specialness that you demand" (T-16.V.10:7). Consciously, we may feel like we are incredibly special, yet beneath that we feel a yawning lack of worth and a brittle sense of self-esteem. So we want to increase our specialness by acquiring someone else's. We want to be somebody else. Who hasn't wanted this? Yet how can we become someone else? It seems impossible, yet it's really rather simple and happens all the time. We give our self away to someone else, we give them our heart, our body, our life. Now it is theirs, and we are relatively free of the burden of that awful thing that never seemed good enough. And in exchange they give us their self, their heart, body, life. It may not be a brain transplant, but the effect is pretty much the same: We feel like a new person.

We give these selves away through a more complete version of the transmission of specialness. To transfer your self to another you simply transfer *all* of your specialness to her. In essence, you give her the deed to your identity. You transfer to her *ownership* of your soul. Sound familiar? This means two things: 1) You give her frequent bodily demonstrations of special devotion; and 2) you give her certain exclusive rights to you. This includes control over the self she now owns, power to decide what it can and cannot do.

In light of this, let us take a fuller look at our love relationships. I start out feeling empty. I attribute this to the fact that my self just isn't special enough. So I go about looking for someone who has a more special self, someone who can grant me abundant specialness. But I cannot expect unlimited specialness, only as much as my self can purchase. So, to catch the best fish possible, I try to enhance my self. I adorn its home, my body, for a special body is a crucial ingredient of a special self. I advertise its strengths and make all its gifts and treasures as visible as possible. And I promise full devotion, full transmittal of my specialness to the lucky winner. All the while, I look carefully for the person who is my best bet; the one who is more special than I, yet who still will strangely consider me more special than she, or who will at least consider my brand of specialness preferable to hers.

When I find this person and she finds me, we arrange for a trade. I sacrifice my self for her. I use all the specialness I have to give her the message that she is special. I give her frequent bodily demonstrations of special devotion and give her control over my self. In so doing I subtly make her responsible for the loss of my self (even though I never liked this self much). This obligates her to give me her self in return.

> Through the death [the sacrifice] of your self you think you can attack [make guilty] another self, and snatch it from the other to replace the self that you despise (T-16.V.10:6).

And as she gives me her self, I pay her back by further gifts of my self. In this way I atone for my own guilt over the loss of her self.

It sounds like a nice business arrangement. "Where both partners see this special self in each other, the ego sees 'a union made in Heaven'" (T-16.V.8:3). If both of us feel like we are acquiring a self that is more special than the one with which we started, then our anger over having to sacrifice our original self will not be so great. And our guilt over "the 'sin' of taking, and of giving nothing of value in return" (T-16.V.7:6), will not be too great, either. And we will be happy.

Hate in disguise

Well, not quite happy. For this whole transaction should look eerily familiar by now. I accuse you of guilt over the loss of my specialness and demand that you restore my loss. Have we not seen this activity before? Strangely enough, this is the exact activity that we identified before as *hate*. There, I accused you of stealing my specialness and demanded that you cough it up and restore it to me. Here, I give you a gift, the gift of my self. And even though this is supposedly a loving gift, it actually puts me in a position to "justifiably" give you the same hateful message: "You are guilty of the loss of my specialness and I am justified in demanding it back." For now you really do have what I lost. I know—I gave it to you.

In special love, then, we are doing the same thing as in hate! We are, in fact, doing the only thing the ego ever motivates us to do, projecting guilt to acquire specialness.

What we call hate and what we call love, then, are the same thing. There is only one thing that makes special love look different than hate: the illusion of giving. I am giving you all kinds of wonderful gifts, as you are me. We are smiling, laughing, hugging, kissing. So much giving is going on, so much loving. Yet, as we have seen, the giving is not real. The only reason I give is that doing so gives me the right to demand a gift in return. It places you in debt to me. It sets you up for my accusation: "You are guilty of my loss. Pay up!"

As difficult and unpleasant as this sounds, this is the message behind almost all of what we call giving. As we said earlier, we wish we could just receive all the goodies without having to pay anything out. Thus somewhere inside we resent having to give, we are angry about it. And a gift that one is angry about giving is really just the gift of anger. As with all anger, this is designed to instill guilt, which in turn is meant to obligate the other to give back.

All of this becomes plainly visible when one of the partners stops giving, stops transmitting his specialness. Now the disguise (along with the gloves) comes off. The illusion of love vanishes and hate steps in unadorned. You have dropped your pretense of special love and so I drop mine. I move in and attack with pure hate: "Here I have sacrificed for you. I have given you my very self. And what did you do? You just kept it and did not give anything back. You are guilty of stealing my self. Give me your self this instant or I'll call my lawyer!"

Obviously, the switch from special love to raw hate does not come all at once. It happens in little ways all the time, as one of us feels that the other has not held up his or her end of the bargain, even slightly. The ways in which we then revert to open hate can be varied and quite subtle. One way is that I get depressed, which seems to be my own internal matter, but which is actually a communication to you.

> In looking at the special relationship, it is necessary first to realize that it involves a great amount of pain. Anxiety, despair, guilt and attack all enter into it, broken into by periods in which they seem to be gone. All these must be understood for what they are. Whatever form they take, they are always an attack on the self to make the other guilty (T-16.V.1:1-4).

Another way is I get sick, which again seems to be something other than the attack on you it is intended to be.

> A sick and suffering you but represents your brother's guilt; the witness that you send lest he forget the injuries he gave, from which you swear he never will escape (T-27.I.4:3).

The point here is that special love is a pure illusion. It is not love. When it is replaced by hate, all that is happening is that the disguise is being removed to reveal what was there all along. True, as we said, some weak reflection of real love is almost always interlaced in our relationships, but this love is the gifts we give with no strings attached. Our bargain-based love is not love. It is this illusory nature of special love that makes it so unstable and temporary. This is why our relationships are so volatile, and ever-changing, and why we switch companions so often.

Because of guilt, all special relationships have
elements of fear in them. This is why they shift and change
so frequently. They are not based on changeless love
alone. And love, where fear has entered, cannot be
depended on because it is not perfect (T-15.V.4:1-4).

The special love partner is acceptable only as long as he
serves [his] purpose. Hatred can enter, and indeed is
welcome in some aspects of the relationship, but it is still
held together by the illusion of love. If the illusion goes,
the relationship is broken or becomes unsatisfying on the
grounds of disillusionment.
Love is not an illusion. It is a fact. Where
disillusionment is possible, there was not love but hate.
For hate is an illusion, and what can change was never
love (T-16.IV.3:5-4:4).

What do we really obtain in the special love relationship? We find
what our egos were really looking for all along. Rather than worth, we find
lack, for, as mentioned earlier, searching outside ourselves for completion
only affirms that completion is outside of us, not within. Rather than
joining, we find loneliness, for the ego all along was using the relationship
to reinforce our separateness.

...an unholy relationship is based on differences, where
each one thinks the other has what he has not. They come
together, each to complete himself and rob the other. They
stay until they think that there is nothing left to steal, and
then move on. And so they wander through a world of
strangers, unlike themselves, living with their bodies
perhaps under a common roof that shelters neither; in the
same room and yet a world apart (T-22.IN.2:5-8).

And rather than innocence, we find guilt, the guilt of degrading our
brother by seeing him as a separate being and by seeing him as a body; the
guilt of attacking him and trying to wrest from his body his "treasure" of
specialness; and the guilt of conditional giving. In fact, according to the
Course, it is guilt, not love, that is actually what attracts us in the special
relationship. On the surface, we are attracted by what looks like love, and

that surface attraction is an important motivator. But underneath that, we are unconsciously excited by the promise that this person is going to make us feel really guilty, for it is guilt that cements our unstable ego into a sense of greater permanence. "Guilt is the only need the ego has, and as long as you identify with it, guilt will remain attractive to you" (T-15.VII.10:4).

> ...the ego really believes that it can get and keep by making guilty. This is its one attraction; an attraction so weak that it would have no hold at all, except that no one recognizes it. For the ego always seems to attract through love, and has no attraction at all to anyone who perceives that it attracts through guilt (T-15.VII.2:5-7).

Giving

What is the alternative to bargaining? It is giving, real giving, that makes no demands for return, that grants complete freedom to the receiver. We will find love only by offering the real thing.

> Forget not this; to bargain is to set a limit, and any brother with whom you have a limited relationship, you hate (T-21.III.1:3).

> Have mercy on yourself who bargains thus. God gives and does not ask for recompense. There is no giving but to give like Him (S-2.II.6:6-7).

> Love is freedom. To look for it by placing yourself in bondage is to separate yourself from it. For the Love of God, no longer seek for union in separation, nor for freedom in bondage! As you release, so will you be released. Forget this not, or love will be unable to find you and comfort you (T-16.VI.2).

> It is not the function of God's teachers to evaluate the outcome of their gifts. It is merely their function to give them. Once they have done that they have also given the outcome, for that is part of the gift. No one can give if he is concerned with the result of giving. That is a limitation

on the giving itself, and neither the giver nor the receiver would have the gift. Trust is an essential part of giving; in fact, it is the part that makes sharing possible, the part that guarantees the giver will not lose, but only gain. Who gives a gift and then remains with it, to be sure it is used as the giver deems appropriate? Such is not giving but imprisoning.

It is the relinquishing of all concern about the gift that makes it truly given (M-6.3:1-4:1).

The Course's philosophy of giving could easily occupy a book. I am not going to go deeply into it here, but the essence of it is that by giving, freely and unconditionally, we receive, rather than lose. We do not receive in the sense of the other person giving back, but simply because giving opens up our awareness to the presence of the gifts within us, making us aware of our inner wellspring of love, worth, innocence, and holiness. The act of giving proves to us the reality of that wellspring. Also, by giving simply out of interest in the other person, we experience a joining with him. We become aware of our common unity, even if the other person still believes he is separate.

Just imagine, if you will, being in a relationship in which your only function was to give to the other person, with no expectation or demand. Imagine being married to someone, for instance, without any bargaining, overt or covert. No deals made that if I do this you will do that. No anger when you do not hold up your "end." No attachment to you performing properly or even staying around because you "owe" it to me. No gauging my giving to make sure I am filling my "giving-quota," or inspecting your giving to see if you are filling yours. No expectation that you will be grateful for what I give. Just giving to you as the natural expression of my being as it looks on the natural beauty of your being. Leaving you totally free to do as you please, requiring nothing of you except to remain the Son of God that you eternally are.

~4~
Shadow Figures from the Past

So far we have seen at the base of our normal, friendly relationships an insanity that we probably would never have dreamed is there. Yet we still have not reached the bottom of it. We have learned that we are not relating to the person in front of us, but merely to our fantasy version of her. Yet, the Course teaches, it is worse than that. We are not relating to our fantasy of *her*, but our fantasy of someone else. She simply reminds us of the past and as we look on her we are really seeing, hearing and interacting with our fantasy image of someone from our past.

The Course points out many times that the special relationship is based on the past.

> The past is the ego's chief learning device, for it is in the past that you learned to define your own needs and acquire methods for meeting them on your own terms (T-15.V.2:1).

How, then, did we learn to meet our needs? By seeking "to separate out certain aspects of the totality and look to them to meet your imagined needs..." (T-15.V.2:3). Yet, "How can you decide that special aspects of the Sonship can give you more than others? The past has taught you this" (T-15.V.3:5-6).

In other words, in the past we decided that we were separate beings, that as separate beings specialness fulfills us, and that certain people can make us feel more special than others. Once we learn that certain individuals make us "happier," we continually—though generally unconsciously—seek out people like them. We are all aware of doing this. For instance, there is the old line, "I want a girl just like the girl that married dear ol' dad."

Yet I think what generally does not occur to us is that by seeking people that remind us of past sources of love, we are really relating to a fantasy image in our minds, rather than the person in front of us; an image that may have as little to do with the past as it does with the present.

Perhaps you think it is your childhood home that you would find again. The childhood of your body, and its place of shelter, are a memory now so distorted that you merely hold a picture of a past that never happened (W-pI.182.4:1-2).

The shadow figures

The Course, however, places much more importance on another highly related phenomenon. This is what it calls the "shadow figures," which the Course discusses in three sections in the Text: 13.IV, 13.V, 17.III (the concept behind shadow figures is also discussed in 16.VII, and the term is mentioned again briefly in 29.IV.5:6). The importance of these discussions is often overlooked because it is hard to discern just what the Course means by "shadow figures."

Shadow figures, just as the term sounds, are mental ghosts. They are mental images of *particular people* from our past, people who still live in our minds as sources of pain, with whom we occasionally hold inner dialogues, whom we project onto current partners, to whom we still have something to prove. In short, they are mental ghosts of people who did not give us the specialness we craved. And because no one gave us *everything* we wanted—since no one made us perfectly happy—everyone from our past to some degree fits into this category. I think, however, that the main people in this category were those who loom largest in our minds: people who seriously mistreated or neglected us, or people from whom we expected so much that it was impossible for them to deliver. There is little doubt that parents place at or near the top of most shadow figure rosters.

Our strategy here is obvious. We feel that the past wounded us and we would desperately like to heal those wounds. But the past is gone. It cannot be changed. What, then, to do? We will bring the past into the present. We will put on a play that re-enacts the past. This time, however, we will change the ending. This time there will be a happy ending. We will be the hero, we will get the love and recognition denied us the first time around. All injustices will be rectified, all wrongs made right, and we will be redeemed.

...the special relationship is an attempt to re-enact the past and change it. Imagined slights, remembered pain, past disappointments, perceived injustices and deprivations all enter into the special relationship, which becomes a way in which you seek to restore your wounded self-esteem (T-16.VII.1:2-3).

By seeking to correct the past, we are really trying to show the shadow figures which haunt our mental attic that they were wrong about us. We are trying to prove that we did not deserve the treatment they gave us. In other words, we are seeking vengeance on them. "The special relationship takes vengeance on the past" (T-16.VII.2:1). "The shadowy figures from the past...carry the spots of pain in your mind, directing you to attack in the present in retaliation for the past that is no more" (T-13.IV.6:1,3). "In the special relationship it does not seem to be an acting out of vengeance that you seek. And even when the hatred and the savagery break briefly through, the illusion of love is not profoundly shaken" (T-16.VII.5:2). Our relationships do not seem vengeance-based merely because we choose not to see that they are.

This process of bringing back the past, says the Course, is universally present in all of our special relationships. We need not be consciously thinking about the past for this process to be occurring. "No special relationship is experienced in the present. Shades of the past envelop it, and make it what it is. It has no meaning in the present..." (T-16.VII.2:3-5). "There is no fantasy that does not contain the dream of retribution for the past" (T-16.VII.4:2). In other words, all that we have talked about thus far in terms of the special relationship needs to be viewed in this light. Let us, therefore, take the themes of the last three chapters and see how these look in light of our attachment to the past.

Selecting a special love partner

In Chapter 2 we talked about the process of selecting a companion. What we did not mention is that the shadow figures guide this selection. In picking a partner we are really casting for the part of our shadow figures in our re-enactment of the past. We select those people who remind us of the shadow figures and who we think will allow us to take revenge on the shadow figures. For example, if our father never gave us the love we wanted, we will be prone to find someone who is like our father. He need not be just like our father. He just needs to be related in some way that allows us to associate him with our father, "no matter how distorted the associations by which you arrive at the connection may be" (T-17.III.2:5). This allows us to project our shadowy image of our father onto him; it allows him to "play" our father. While with this person, we will try to get him to give us the love our father never gave us. We will try to get him to do it right this time. He will be the one who pays for the sins of our father.

> What basis would you have for choosing a special partner without the past? Every such choice is made because of something "evil" in the past to which you cling [an "evil" done to you], and for which must someone else [the new partner] atone (T-16.VII.1:4-5).

As disturbing as this pattern is, we can all see it in our own lives. We can see it in the frequent thoughts we have that say, "See, this proves that you were wrong about me." We can see it in destructive relationships that we repeat over and over again with new names but with the same patterns; new faces but somehow the same partner. Or when we wake up after years of pain in a relationship and realize that all along we were really responding not to the person in front of us, but to our mother or father. Sometimes we are taking revenge on particular people; sometimes on whole classes of people from the past. Either way, we are a ship anchored in the harbor of the past.

Relating to a fantasy

One of the more disturbing things the Course says about our relationships is that we are not really relating to the people in front of us, but are having a private interaction with the shadow figures we have projected onto them. Thus, when we hear our partner speak we are "hearing" the shadow figure speak to us, and when we respond we are speaking to the shadow figure.

> In effect, if you follow the ego's dictates you will react to your brother as though he were someone else, and this will surely prevent you from recognizing him as he is. And you will receive messages from him out of your own past

because, by making it real in the present, you are forbidding yourself to let it go (T-13.IV.5:5-6).

This adds another dimension onto our discussion in Chapter 2. There we talked about the process of shutting out the reality of our companion and substituting for that an image that we make in our minds. At the end of this process we obtained an image of him or her that is simply a collection of preferred body parts. In light of our current topic, this process takes one sad step farther:

> In the unholy relationship, it is not the body of the other with which union is attempted, but the bodies of those [the shadow figures] who are not there. For even the body of the other, already a severely limited perception of him, is not the central focus as it is, or in entirety. What [body parts] can be used for fantasies of vengeance, and what [parts] can be most readily associated with those on whom vengeance is really sought, is centered on and separated off as being the only parts of value. Every step taken in the making, the maintaining and the breaking off of the unholy relationship is a move toward further fragmentation and unreality. The shadow figures enter more and more, and the one in whom they seem to be decreases in importance (T-17.III.3).

In other words, the body parts of our partner that we focus on are those that can best "be used for fantasies of vengeance." They are the parts that most readily remind us of "those on whom vengeance is really sought." We are not relating to the person in front of us but to a set of special body parts. And we are not even relating to *their* parts, but to the parts of someone who is not even there.

This draws us to a sobering conclusion. Since the past is gone, if I am relating to it, I am relating to no one. I am talking to myself. I am lost in my own private world, and that is the definition of insanity. An insane person is someone who has conjured up his own reality and relates to it, rather than to reality. This is precisely what we are doing.

> Thus do they communicate with those who are not there, and it is they who answer them. And no one hears their

answer save him who called upon them, and he alone
believes they answered him (T-13.V.3:3-4).

As you look with open eyes upon your world, it must
occur to you that you have withdrawn into insanity. You
see what is not there, and you hear what makes no
sound....You communicate with no one, and you are as
isolated from reality as if you were alone in all the
universe. In your madness you overlook reality
completely... (T-13.V.6:1-5).

Attacking with guilt to gain specialness

In Chapters 1 and 3 we discussed the ego's single activity in
relation to others. This is essentially a vengeance process whereby I accuse
you of stealing my specialness and demand it back. Seeing this activity in
light of our preoccupation with the past can give us our most complete view
yet of the special relationship.

In the past I wanted to acquire the specialness that I saw as residing
in your body. I wanted your body to yield up this specialness to me. But it
did not happen and this left a scar in my mind. So now my image of you is a
ghost that haunts the dark hallways of my mind. I therefore am driven to re-
enact the past and turn the tables on you. To do so I find someone that can
play the part of you in my little psychodrama. If I can get this person to give
me what you withheld, then I have taken revenge on you. I have proven you
were wrong and have recovered from you (through the actor playing you)
what you stole. I may try to forcibly wrench from this person the
specialness I want. I may try to finesse it out of her with gifts. I may
attack her body or make love to it. But whatever I do I will be (overtly or
covertly) attacking her to instill guilt in order to seize from her body its
treasure of specialness. And, of course, all the while I will really be
seeing her as a stand-in for you. I will really be attacking you, stealing
from *your* body, proving *you* wrong. In my little fantasy, you will be
paying me your debt through her. And since this is pretty much all I do,
you might say that my whole life is one big psychodrama, but for the
sake of revenge, not for healing.

Why bring back the dead?

If the past is gone for good, why do we keep bringing it back? How can you change the past except in fantasy? And who can give you what you think the past deprived you of? The past is nothing. Do not seek to lay the blame for deprivation on it, for the past is gone. You cannot really not let go what has already gone. It must be, therefore, that you are maintaining the illusion that it has not gone because you think it serves some purpose that you want fulfilled (T-16.VII.2:6-11).

The Course implies that the idea of gaining revenge for my specialness is not the deepest cause of my bringing back the past. There is some more fundamental attempt being made. What I am really trying to do is two-fold:

Keep the past, and thus the ego, going. In the past I attacked and was attacked. This is the kind of stuff the ego loves. This is what keeps it in business. It does not want me to *solve* this, but to keep it going. If it can keep me repeating the past, I will continue feeling guiltier and more wounded; I will become more and more convinced that I am an ego. Also, the past is where the ego was conceived. The more the past is re-run, the more the ego is frozen in time, perpetually preserved.

Defend against the present and the holy encounter. Remember, what we really fear is the dissolution of the ego. It is only in the present that this can happen. The present is within time, but is not really *of* time. It is actually a tiny shard of eternity. It is here that we can let go of the past, and here that we can experience timelessness. Our brother is also a tiny fragment of infinity. In joining with him we feel a foretaste of Heaven. And of course, this holy encounter can only take place in the present. Otherwise, we "join" with only an image in our minds, and so encounter no one. Therefore, the ego is heavily invested in keeping us out of the present.

Now is the closest approximation of eternity that this world offers. It is in the reality of "now," without past or future, that the beginning of the appreciation of eternity lies. For only "now" is here, and only "now" presents the opportunities for the holy encounters in which salvation can be found (T-13.IV.7:5-7).

We will return to this theme of entering the present in Chapter 6.

~5~
The Ultimate Shadow Figure

*I*n this chapter we hit the bedrock level of the special relationship. In what I think is one of the most important and difficult sections in the Course, "The Choice for Completion," it is revealed that the special relationship is really intended as an attack on God. In the last chapter we saw that the person in front of us is just a symbol for someone from our past. However, that person is not the end of the line. He, in turn, is just a symbol for God, a god that we made up. Thus, we are using the person in the present to get back at someone from our past. And we are using that person from the past to get back at God. Whenever we try to make someone guilty, either with direct attack or with "gifts," we are seeking to make God guilty. We are taking revenge on God. This is the core, the subterranean foundation, of the special relationship.

> Very simply, the attempt to make guilty is always directed against God. For the ego would have you see Him, and Him alone, as guilty... (T-16.V.2:1-2).

This fact is obviously completely outside of our conscious awareness. How could it be true? Let us attempt to trace the logic by which we arrived at our use of relationships to attack God.

The Course suggests that the roots of the separation go back to a request to be made special. "You were at peace until you asked for special favor" (T-13.III.10:2). Imagine that you are part of an endless sea of awareness, and the entire sea is basking in the sunlight of its Creator. Your joy over being part of this sea and soaking in the warmth of the Creator is infinite. Somehow—and here I am simply speculating—a thought comes into your mind: "Could there be more?" And the answer comes, "Instead of being simply part of this sea, instead of being loved by the Creator the same as all other parts, what if I were special? What if the Creator loved me more than any other single part? What if I were His favorite? Now, *that* would be more." So you asked the Creator, "Father, please single me out. Please love me more."

> To "single out" is to "make alone," and thus make lonely. God did not do this to you. Could He set you apart, knowing that your peace lies in His Oneness? He denied you only your request for pain, for suffering is not of His creation (T-13.III.12:1-4).

It is God's Nature to give only Love that is impartial, non-selective, undifferentiated, to shine His Love out freely and impersonally in all directions, to give its total measure away to each member of His Kingdom. To single you out would be to cut you off and thereby give you *less*, not more. And He could not do that. God knows nothing of loss and pain.

Yet it was too late. You had already become attached to the ego, the illusion of separateness. You decided to strike out on your own and find the treasure that was so great that God had to make it forbidden. With illusion heavy on your eyes, you sank into a world of dreams, in which as a separate self you could seek the ultimate prize of specialness. In your new world it was specialness that was needed above all. It was "the secret ingredient that would give meaning to your life" (T-23.II.12:9). Yet seek as you might, you never felt special enough. This was clearly God's fault. If only God had made you special. If only He had exalted you to the status of favorite son. Then your specialness would have been an eternal fact, a pillar in the halls of reality.

To make matters worse, your very existence as a separate self seemed only partly real. This self of yours was clearly weak, vulnerable and impermanent. Clearly God must not have granted it the permanent reality that only He could give. And so your new self felt flimsy and insubstantial. A long, burning anger began smoldering within you. God would not make your ego real! "While the ego is...unaware of spirit, it does perceive itself as being rejected by something greater than itself" (T-4.II.8:8). Even through your closed eyes your ego sensed the looming threat of God's Love, a Love so intensely bright that one look on it and the ego would be vaporized.

Since God is the all-powerful Creator, had He backed your new venture, it would have been a great success. But since He did not, He was the reason your existence never seemed to work. He was responsible for your wobbly sense of identity. He was responsible for how average and mediocre you were, for how un-special you felt. And now His non-special Love represented a constant, immanent threat to your whole reality.

Your dilemma was this: While God's reality and His Love remain intact, your illusions (of separateness and specialness) are denied reality and constantly threatened with dissolution. There must be a way to take reality and power away from God and *transfer* it to you, leaving God helpless and infusing your separateness/specialness with eternal vitality. There had to be a way to take life away from God and give it to your illusions; a way for the ego to steal the treasure from God's inner sanctum, to eat the forbidden fruit, to steal fire from Heaven. This way, of course, is the special love relationship.

> It is in the special relationship, born of the hidden wish for special love from God, that the ego's hatred triumphs. For the special relationship is the renunciation of the Love of God, and the attempt to secure for the self the specialness that He denied (T-16.V.4:1-2).

> To the ego completion lies in triumph, and in the extension of the "victory" even to the final triumph over God. In this it sees the ultimate freedom of the self, for nothing would remain to interfere with the ego (T-16.V.5:5-6).

How does the special relationship accomplish all this? It is accomplished in the self trade we discussed in Chapter 4. This trade, if you recall, is one in which you sacrifice your self, thus attacking another with guilt so that he will give you his more special self.

> Through the death of your self you think you can attack another self, and snatch it from the other to replace the self that you despise. And you despise it because you do not think it offers the specialness that you demand (T-16.V.10:6-7).

As we said earlier, by sacrificing your self, you are making an "attack on the self to make the other guilty" (T-16.V.1:4). But the real target of your guilt is not your partner; it is God, for, as was quoted above, "the attempt to make guilty is always directed against God." What you are doing is sending a hate message to God, which says, "Look at this un-special, good-for-nothing self I have. You're the one to blame for me having this thing. To show how guilty You are, I am going to just throw it away; I am going to kill it." And that is what you do when you give your self away to another. You symbolically kill it as an expression of your disgust with it, with its lack of specialness which you blame on God. You send a message to God, showing Him how guilty He is for giving you a self not worth keeping.

Now comes the real victory. For when your special love partner actually gives you his special self, you have *acquired* what God denied. And since God is the Ruler of the universe, you have actually stolen it right out of God's Hands. In fact, deep in your unconscious you have projected the shadow figure of God onto your partner. He or she is wearing the mask of God in your primitive ritual, playing the role of God in your mythic re-enactment of the dawn of time. Your partner giving you specialness is "really" God finally surrendering to you what He originally refused.

You have therefore defeated God. You are the winner. His Life, His status, His power, has drained out of Him, leaving Him and His divine Love disempowered, dead. And it has transferred to you, leaving you and your specialness on His throne, eternally alive and triumphant. Having stolen fire right out of His Hands, you now wear His Crown. Having eaten the forbidden fruit, you are a god. You have what you always sought: Your specialness is eternally real, and the threat of God is forever vanquished.

> The central theme in [the special relationship's] litany to sacrifice is that God must die so you can live...[so you can] endow the little self you made with power you wrested from truth, triumphing over it and leaving it helpless (T-16.V.10:4, 11:3).

In other words, God is the ultimate shadow figure. He is the One from your past that did not give you the specialness you craved. And now through your special love partner, you gain vengeance on Him. You go back and change that primordial past, proving Him wrong and seizing the specialness He denied. Your special love partner, then, is a kind of voodoo doll representing God; whatever you do to him you magically do to God. When you sacrifice yourself to make your partner guilty, you are sticking a pin in the voodoo doll, making God reel with guilt. When you snatch the specialness out of the body of your partner, the heavens shake as God feels His vitality leave His Body. And as you take hold of the precious special love, God watches His entire Kingdom—founded on non-special, universal

Love—teeter and begin to crumble. Your victory is complete. You have stolen reality away from Heaven and used it to light the lamps of your illusions.

The special relationship, then, is a tantrum we throw in response to the ultimate authority problem. We are adolescents who, sensing that our formless Dad has forbidden us specific love, have to rebelliously acquire it in order to establish our own separate identity. Special love is the ultimate weapon in a metaphysical Oedipal war, by which we steal from our Father the romantic treasure that He has possessively withheld from us.

The Course does not intend all this as simply a shocking but ultimately fictional story. Somewhere deep in the vaults of our minds, these dynamics are actually at work. And, rising up in disguised form, they are what is actually responsible for what this world calls "love." Our ego really "does perceive itself as being rejected by something greater than itself" (T-4.II.8:8). It somehow senses the presence of a non-dual realm which threatens its existence by virtue of this realm being more real and being totally ego-alien. The ego wants to defeat this realm and give solidity and permanence to itself. And it uses our relationships to accomplish this.

To make this more real, think about the following scenario. You have fallen hopelessly in love with someone, though you have no idea if this person is in love with you. Then one night he or she looks deeply into your eyes and says, "You are the most special person in the world to me." In the resulting exhilaration, I suspect that the following things are probably true. Somewhere inside you realize that this person has given you the sense of worth (read "specialness") that God never has (for if He had made you special enough, you would never have needed to give your self away to your new partner). And in this same place inside of you, something says, "This is it. This is happiness. Why seek anywhere else for my treasure, when I have found it right here. I don't need to transcend my ego, to change my whole way of perceiving the world. I don't need to awaken to God, for I have found Heaven on earth. I have all that I could need right here." As we said earlier, the special relationship is the ego's best defense against Heaven.

Is it so hard to imagine, then, that just a little deeper in your mind these thoughts are going on: "Through this wonderful creature's eyes, fingers and lips, I have finally managed to wrench from God the specialness He would never give me. I no longer need to worry about Him sucking me into His formless Heaven, for I have stolen His power and used it to empower my specialness and make *it* god"? His reality has been defeated and your illusions made forever real.

This whole thing is absolutely nuts, is it not? In response to this utter insanity, the Course asks us one very pointed question:

If you perceived the special relationship as a triumph over God, would you want it? (T-16.V.10:1)

How could you want to defeat God? For God is your Eternal Love, "Whose pull is so strong that you cannot resist it" (T-13.II.1:2). "For still deeper than the ego's foundation, and much stronger than it will ever be, is your intense and burning love of God, and His for you" (T-13.III.2:8). If you could just draw aside ever so slightly "the dark cloud that obscures it, your love for your Father would impel you to answer His call and leap into Heaven" (T-13.III.2:6).

We could never want to defeat our Beloved. Thinking that we have done so to Him is the source of all our unhappiness. It is what has given rise to this lonely world of suffering, which is but a

...dream of fierce retaliation for a crime that could not be committed; for attack on what is wholly unassailable. It is a nightmare of abandonment by an Eternal Love, Which could not leave the Son whom It created out of love (W-pI.190.2:4-5).

Thankfully, attack on God is impossible. This is one father that cannot be hurt or angered. Not the entire seeming universe and all its billions of years have caused one breath of disturbance in that eternally calm Mind. "Nothing you can do can change Eternal Love" (C-5.6:10). "God is not angry. He merely could not let this happen. You cannot change His Mind. No rituals that you have set up in which the dance of death delights you can bring death to the eternal" (T-16.V.12:7-10). No matter what we think we have done, the Father waits for us with open Arms, just as in the story of the Prodigal Son:

He was ashamed to return to his father, because he thought he had hurt him. Yet when he came home the father welcomed him with joy, because the son himself was his father's treasure. He wanted nothing else (T-8.VI.4:2-4).

~6~
The Healing of
the Special Relationship

The endless, unrewarding chain
of special relationships

Now that we have all the pieces in place, let us recap the special relationship's time line, from beginning to end. In the beginning, we asked God to make us special. When He wouldn't do this we separated from Him (fell asleep to Him) and made our own world. This world was dedicated to two things: the pursuit of specialness and the relief of our guilt over abandoning God.

To acquire these things we must find someone to symbolically play the role of God, who can accept the guilt that is God's due and grant us the specialness that is *ours*. Finding this person is usually not too difficult: We merely come out of the womb and open our eyes. Mommy and Daddy make perfect God-figures. They are all-powerful beings who exist to supply all of our needs. Their job is to accept responsibility for our happiness and unhappiness. When we are not happy, they are to blame, and we voice our disapproval. This, like an electric collar, gives them the shocks of guilt which are just the motivator they need. As if by magic they are moved to shower us with love, to tell us—with their milk, blankets, hugs, kisses, sparkling eyes and loving words—how special we are. If all goes well, they will be the perfect conduit through which God sends specialness to us, and therefore admits that He was wrong for not doing so in the first place.

But of course parents never do their job quite right, for they invariably fail to give us the sense of infinite specialness we crave. We end up feeling instead that they owe us something, something they refuse to give. We know they haven't given it because we are not happy. We end up feeling the same way towards our teachers, friends, siblings and relatives. All of these people live on in our minds as haunting memories. They have become shadow figures. We talk to them when we are alone, making persuasive cases to them which prove beyond a reasonable doubt that they should have treated us better.

But these internal dialogues never satisfy. So we decide to stage a re-enactment of the past. We try to find the perfect actor to play Mom and/or Dad (and/or teacher, friend, sibling, etc.). This person must fulfill two criteria: She must be really special, and she must remind us somehow of our shadow figures. She will be the one who, wearing the mask of our shadow figures and of God, will give us the specialness they denied. Through her gift they will admit just how wrong they were.

Once we find her, we fall in love not with the person, but with the *promise*, the shining hope that she can supply all that the past withheld from us. Toward this future promise we make eager payments. We compliment her, wine and dine her, do all we can to make her feel special. We give her our self, praying it will be enough. And when we make this giving official and slip that ring on her finger, we believe we receive in return the title to her soul. We think we own her.

Now we can lean back (usually in front of the TV), reduce the payments and reap the benefits of what we purchased. Unfortunately, *she* is thinking the exact same thing, meaning that both of us switch from the "giving" mode to that of waiting for our reward, with the inevitable result that neither of us receive our expected due. Hence we both begin the ominous trend of switching our getting technique from "giving" to "*making guilty*" (T-15.VII.2:5). In our minds we already gave, so we start calling in the debt. We say, in essence, "Look at all I have done for you. Look at all the sacrifices I have made. Did I not give you my very self? Did you not understand the agreement?" We say this out loud, of course, but also in more subtle ways: by lapsing into anxiety, depression, even illness, all of which demonstrate what the other's lovelessness has done to us.

Unless the bargain structure can be repaired, the relationship will spiral downward into harsh recrimination (in both its active and passive forms) and ultimately, separation. The smiling mask of special love will be removed to reveal the glaring face of hate. Even when an acceptable bargain is re-established, each person often ends up feeling alone, resentful and misunderstood. The partner that held such promise has become another bitter disappointment. The one that was supposed to be our sweet revenge on all who didn't love us has become another one to get revenge on. Our love, our darling, our sweetheart has become another shadow figure.

So now we move on. We need not leave her physically. We can find a substitute for her, onto whom we now project *her* face. And the process begins again. There is the new promise of finding the specialness we lack and of establishing the guilt of all those past people who withheld it. There are the new gifts designed to purchase this wonderful outcome. These new gifts then give way to simple blaming, in the hopes that this will forcibly seize the gifts we paid for but have not received. And when this fails, the new love joins the ranks of the ghosts of the past and becomes a new shadow figure.

And on and on it goes. Each new person wears an ever-increasing pile of masks, masks of former spouses and friends, of teachers and parents, and beneath them all the mask of God Himself. Each relationship is a repetition of the last, in only somewhat different form. Each is dedicated to projecting blame in order to acquire specialness. Each begins with instilling guilt through gifts and ends with instilling guilt through simple finger-pointing. No matter how carefully we set this ritual up, it never works. The magic never comes. Or at least it never stays.

> Over and over and over this ritual is enacted. And it is never completed, nor ever will be completed (T-16.V.11:6-7).

This same idea is echoed in the following passage:

> And thus it [the ego] embarks on an endless, unrewarding chain of special relationships, forged out of anger and dedicated to but one insane belief; that the more anger you invest outside yourself, the safer you become (T-15.VII.4:6).

An "endless, unrewarding chain of special relationships." Most of us can agree that this phrase captures the short span of our current lives. Yet how endless has this chain really been? How long have we been searching in the same way for the same elusive treasure which we never find? If you believe the Course when it says that this process started *before* the physical universe was born, it has been a very long time indeed.

How do we get out?

We have been taking a very hard look at the insanity beneath our "sane," "loving" relationships. What do we do about that insanity? Actually, a great deal of the Course's answer lies in exactly what we have been doing: looking at the insanity. The mind is inherently sane, which is why, if it wants to hang onto insanity, it must push that insanity outside of awareness, substituting for it something that appears justifiable and sane. For, once exposed to full awareness, the mind would see insanity as insane and simply reject it.

However, to really be able to look at our egos, we must do so without guilt. Guilt seems to be an honest, objective reaction to the ego, an effort to chase it away. But it is actually the ego judging itself, in an effort to reinforce itself. "Self-blame is...ego identification, and as much an ego defense as blaming others" (T-11.IV.5:5). To get rid of the ego you must be willing to observe it dispassionately, without guilt, telling yourself that it is not you, that it is "meaningless, rather than 'good' or 'bad'" (W-pI.25.5:2).

The holy instant

Though this is an entire topic unto itself, the main answer the Course provides in its discussions of special relationships is the holy instant. The Course openly says, "The holy instant is the Holy Spirit's must useful learning device for teaching you love's meaning [and thus for correcting special love]. For its purpose is to suspend judgment entirely" (T-15.V.1:1-2).

What is a holy instant? The following definition is from my *A Course Glossary*:

> A moment in which we temporarily set aside the past and enter into the timeless present, in which we momentarily transcend identification with illusions and recognize what is real. We enter the holy instant not by making ourselves holy, but by forgetting our normal frame of reference, with its absorption in the past, the future, the body and our own sinfulness. This allows our minds to be still and shift into another state of mind. There we experience the lifting of the barriers of space and time, unawareness of the body, the sudden feeling of peace, joy and love, recognition of our true holiness, and communion with all that seemed to lay outside of us—with all our brothers and with God.

The holy instant may be experienced partially and so not be particularly memorable. Or it may be experienced more totally, in which case we will be lifted out of normal sense perception into a transcendental realm.

Our special relationships are rooted in the past: in our past frame of reference, our judgment of our own needs, our feelings of hurt and our condemnation of others. It is in the past that we learned how to select certain people and exclude others. It was in the past that we learned that we are empty and thus need "to look without and snatch love guiltily from where you thought it was" (T-15.V.9:7). Our whole definition of love as special love, a definition which blocks the true meaning of love, comes from the past.

When we enter fully into the present, several things occur. We leave behind our frame of reference with which we judge. Suddenly, we no longer know what anything means and our minds become open to new meanings. We also realize that the past is gone. We discover that past history does not determine the present, that the present is completely free. We also leave behind our wounds, and with them our resentments, our justifications for attack. The errors and "sins" of our brothers are no longer relevant.

All of this leaves us in a state of mind that allows us to see our brother for who he really is. "When you have learned to look on everyone with no reference at all to the past, either his or yours as you perceive it, you will be able to learn from what you see now" (T-13.VI.2:3). "...you perceive a brother only as you see him *now*. His past has no reality in the present, so you cannot see it" (T-13.VI.1:3-4). "The miracle enables you to see your brother without his past, and so perceive him as born again. His errors are all past, and by perceiving him without them you are releasing him. And since his past is yours, you share in this release" (T-13.VI.5:1-3). "To be born again is to let the past go, and look without condemnation upon the present" (T-13.VI.3:5).

And this, if the holy instant is truly a full one, brings our minds into a state that is truly extraordinary and transcendental. We experience "the lifting of the barriers of time and space, the sudden experience of peace and joy, and, above all, the lack of awareness of the body..." (T-18.VI.13:6). We experience a joining with the entire Sonship, minus all separation, selectivity, exclusion or inequality; and with God, the Creator of the Sonship.

> All your relationships are blessed in the holy instant,
> because the blessing is not limited. In the holy instant the

> Sonship gains as one, and united in your blessing it becomes one to you....in the holy instant you unite directly with God, and all your brothers join in Christ (T-15.V.10).

In the holy instant we learn the true meaning of love, that love is not special or exclusive, but absolutely impartial and all-inclusive.

We have all had holy instants of one sort or another, moments in which we are lifted out of our ordinary state of mind into a condition of exalted happiness, in which the world and everyone in it looked completely different. The Course asks us to use these experiences to our advantage. We do so by comparing the joyous experience of the holy instant, not to our hopes of finding the perfect special love relationship, but to the actual results of our pursuit of special love. This is discussed in a section entitled "The Two Pictures" (which we already referred to in Chapter 2). There the Course calls the special relationship a tiny, dark picture of death (the real content of the relationship), surrounded by a massive, gaudy frame (the appearance and promise of love). The purpose of the frame is to distract our eyes from the picture, while at the same time *framing* the picture, *offering* the picture. It then says,

> Look at the picture. Do not let the frame distract you....Death lies in this glittering gift. Let not your gaze dwell on the hypnotic gleaming of the frame. Look at the picture, and realize that death is offered you (T-17.IV.9).

This, of course, is exactly what we have been doing for the last several chapters: looking at the picture. Then this section begins to talk about the holy instant, saying that the holy instant is a picture of Heaven— better yet, a window onto Heaven—set in a frame of time. Finally, it asks us to compare the two pictures, and this is something we can actually do. We can take the holy instants we have experienced in our lives and compare them with what we really ended up with in our quest for special love. If we do this I believe we will find that our holy instants were far more joyous than our special relationships. The section concludes by saying that if we really compare the two pictures, we will see that the holy instant is not really a picture at all. It is a gateway onto a permanent realm, which can be ours forever if we only are willing to give up the picture of death and its deceptive frame.

Using the holy instant in special relationships

Another place in the Course gives us a specific instruction for using holy instants in our special relationships:

> The Holy Spirit asks only this little help of you: Whenever your thoughts wander to a special relationship which still attracts you, enter with Him into a holy instant, and there let Him release you (T-16.VI.12:1).

I have put together the following exercise which attempts to flesh out this instruction. The exercise is a very confrontive one, which we will often have tremendous resistance to doing. But it also is very transformative.

1. Watch your mind for the attraction of special love
Watch for the following thoughts:

- When are you judging one better, more desirable, than another?
- When are you deciding what your needs are, how to meet them?
- When are you trying to prove to the people of your past that you are better/deserve more than they thought?
- When are you believing that you are lacking and that someone else can make you whole?
- When are you feeling an attraction to bodies?
- When are you planning to pursue/woo/court someone?

2. Be willing to see the pain in these thoughts
When you notice yourself entertaining any of the above thoughts, be willing to see the pain in them right now. Do not wait until they play themselves out months or years from now. Look at the picture now.

- Be willing to see that your attraction will bring not happiness but pain.
- Be willing to see that your attraction is insane, is not love

but an attack.
- Be willing to see that it is really an attraction to guilt, not love, for guilt is what it will inevitably bring.

3. Recognize that a holy instant would make you happier
Recognize that everything you seek for in a special relationship is really found in the holy instant. You may want to read the following passage:

> Hear Him gladly, and learn of Him that you have need of no special relationships at all. You but seek in them what you have thrown away. And through them you will never learn the value of what you have cast aside, but still desire with all your heart. Let us join together in making the holy instant all that there is, by desiring that it be all that there is (T-15.VIII.2:1-4).

4. Enter into a holy instant
Then try to accept a holy instant. Do not be concerned about what you have felt in the past or may feel in the future. Just in that one moment let go of your normal frame of reference and desire that the holy instant be given you.

- Be willing for an instant to completely step aside from your attractions/strategies/feelings/perspectives.
- Desire the love, peace and unlimited communication of the holy instant.
- If it helps you, ask Jesus to step between you and your fantasies, as he says he will do:

> My holy brother, I would enter into all your relationships, and step between you and your fantasies (T-17.III.10:1).

In accepting a holy instant it may help to repeat one of these prayers from the Text, holding each word in full awareness, meaning the words as much as you can, and repeating the prayer many times if necessary:

Your part is only to remember this; you do not want anything you value to come of a relationship. You choose neither to hurt it nor to heal it in your own way....Focus your mind only on this:

I am not alone, and I would not intrude the past upon
my Guest.
I have invited Him, and He is here.
I need do nothing except not to interfere (T-16.I.3).

I give you to the Holy Spirit as part of myself.
I know that you will be released,
unless I want to use you to imprison myself.
In the name of my freedom I choose your release,
because I recognize that we will be released together
(T-15.XI.10:5-7).

Please note: the above exercise is not meant to imply that we should reject all relationships, or that we should avoid anyone we feel attracted to. It is not the relationship that we are meant to transcend, but the attraction to specialness. Our relationships are our salvation, but they save us as we face and relinquish our attraction to feeling special, in favor of our attraction to holiness.

Forgiveness

The holy instant is the instant when forgiveness happens. That is why it is so central in healing the special relationship. Forgiveness is the letting go of the past. The holy instant is a moment when we let go of the past. The two concepts go hand-in-hand.

Forgiveness is the Course's method of salvation from the human condition. And since the special relationship is what keeps the human condition cemented in place, forgiveness is also our salvation from the special relationship. This makes perfect sense if you reflect on it. The special relationship is a *demand* that someone else save me through behaving toward me in certain special ways, and the *resentment* that results when he or she does not. Instead of redoubling our efforts to wring the "right" behaviors out of our partner, forgiveness lets it all go. We realize that his or her sin was only an illusion, a distortion in our own perception. And so we forgive our brother "for what he did not do" (T-17.III.1:5).

To truly let it all go, we must release our brother not only for his "sin" of not fulfilling the role we set for him. We must also liberate him from the role as well, from all the agendas, expectations and demands we placed on him. Forgiveness releases the entire sense of need we had in relation to him. It gives up our perception of him as an individual entity encased in a body, a body that fulfilled or denied our needs through certain special body parts.

> What is your brother for? You do not know, because your function is obscure to you. Do not ascribe a role to him that you imagine would bring happiness to you. And do not try to hurt him when he fails to take the part that you assigned to him, in what you dream your life was meant to be (T-29.IV.6:1-4).

When forgiveness is complete we do not see our brother as someone who is there to meet our needs. We see only an opportunity to give, for we have realized that giving love is the only real need we have. We finally perceive that happiness comes not from getting anything from anyone, but simply from shining the light of our love to everyone we meet, or see, or think of. When this is our purpose behind every interaction, the people we encounter will look entirely different, as the following passage states:

> A shadow figure who attacks becomes a brother giving you a chance to help, if this becomes the function of the dream. And dreams of sadness thus are turned to joy (T-29.IV.5:6-7).

This is clearly a very high state: releasing all the "wrongs" that were ever done against us, releasing all the demands we ever placed on anyone, and being interested only in giving, without limit or partiality. How do we reach this place? I do not think there is anything that is going to magically do it for us. Reaching this place is the spiritual journey itself. Forgiveness, then, is not a gimmick or a quick fix. It is a life journey. So if you want to realize it, give yourself entirely to the spiritual path. And if *A Course in Miracles* is your path, then give yourself entirely to it. Study it as if its words literally held the hidden key to your salvation. Practice its lessons as if they could actually bring you the peace you have always wanted. And extend this peace to others as if giving it to them was the only way you could truly receive it yourself. If you want to know forgiveness, real, unconditional forgiveness, then study it, practice it and extend it, as if your happiness depended on it. See this as your life purpose, rather than a mere hobby you do on the side.

What, then, do you do with all your special relationships, which you now realize were formed to perpetuate your madness? See them as the perfect classrooms in which you learn real forgiveness. That is what they are for. They are not there to meet all your so-called needs. Be grateful that they will inevitably frustrate your hopes and dreams, for then you are given the perfect opportunity to learn real forgiveness. And when your partner does what seems to be unforgivable, realize that this is the very situation forgiveness was made for. You may even use the Workbook prayer, *"Let this help me learn what forgiveness means"* (W-pI.rII.81.4:2). By not turning to your old methods to relieve your pain you are offering your relationships to the Holy Spirit to use for His purpose, for forgiveness *is* His purpose. This change of purpose is the first step in making your relationships holy:

> However unholy the reason you made [your relationships] may be, He can translate them into holiness by removing as much fear as you will let Him. You can place any relationship under His care and be sure that it will not result in pain, if you offer Him your willingness to have it serve no need but His (T-15.V.5:3-4).

Part Two

Holy
Relationships

Introduction
to Part Two

*T*he topic of holy relationships is an extremely important one in *A Course in Miracles*. It would be difficult to overestimate its importance. I think we often forget that the Course was born out of the holy relationship of its scribes, Helen Schucman and Bill Thetford. If you are familiar with the story, you know that the Course came out of a joining they had experienced, and in turn was intended to heal their relationship. In a sense, therefore, the holiness of their relationship was both the birthplace and the goal of the Course.

The holy relationship also figures prominently in the actual pages of the Course. In the Text, it is a major running theme for well over a hundred pages (amounting to about a fifth of the Text), beginning in Chapter 17 and running through Chapter 22, with a few final mentions in 23 and 24. Here, Helen and Bill were given specific instruction in how their holy relationship could achieve its goal, instruction that now applies to every holy relationship. In the Manual for Teachers, the idea pops up again. In fact, the holy relationship between teacher and pupil is a keynote of the Manual (see especially M-2.5, 3.1-5, 4.1). And we find the theme again in the pages of the *Psychotherapy* pamphlet (see P-2.IN.4, 2.I.3, 2.II.5-9), in which we are told that establishing a holy relationship between therapist and patient is the key to successful therapy. Lastly, the idea crops up (by concept but not by name) in *The Song of Prayer* (see S-1.IV.1-3), in the notion of two people joining in prayer.

All in all, the holy relationship gets more press in the Course than the special relationship, if one can believe that. And even though the Course is usually described as a self-study course, it is very much in keeping with the Course to walk its path together, in pairs or in groups. It was intended that Helen and Bill practice it together, and, according to the Manual, it is also intended that Course teachers join with new students in practicing it together. When the Manual says that teacher and pupil are supposed to "learn the same course" (M-2.5:7), the same spiritual path, this primarily refers to learning *A Course in Miracles* together. For the Manual itself "is a manual for a special curriculum, intended for teachers of a special form of the universal course" (M-1.4:1). In other words, it is a manual for teachers of the Course, who will join with pupils of the Course in learning the Course.

Yet despite the importance of this topic of holy relationships, I think it is an extremely neglected and little understood topic among Course students. In my experience, the impression most students have of what a holy relationship is comes mainly from the words "holy relationship" themselves, from what those words sound like they must mean. In other words, given our understanding of the Course's overall thought system, we assume that the words "holy" "relationship" must clearly be such-and-such. In my mind this amounts to projecting our own meaning onto those words, rather than discovering what the author of the Course actually meant by them.

What I think is especially unrecognized is the fact that the Course has a very developed vision of the holy relationship, described in detail over dozens of sections (which means there is really no need to guess at what the author meant by the term). In the end, it sketches a whole progression through which the relationship goes on the way from its beginning to the achievement of its goal. I have arranged the chapters in Part II of this book to reflect the stages of this progression.

To qualify things a little: You may get the impression from the following that there can be only one holy relationship in your life, and that it will be a male-female relationship. That is not the case. You may have several holy relationships, and they certainly can be with someone of the same sex.

Also, I do not think that everything said in this book or in the Course accurately describes *every* holy relationship. So if a relationship in your life qualifies as holy according to the Course's criteria (which we will discuss in Chapter 1), yet does not sound too much like what you read in here, do not be too shaken. The holy relationship takes many different forms and Part II of this book will primarily speak to those forms that are similar to Helen and Bill's, since their relationship is the one directly addressed in the Text discussions. Perhaps the best way to put it is that the more significant and long-term the relationship is, the more this book will probably apply to it.

As I said, the Course describes a basic progression which the holy relationship passes through. And though this progression may not completely apply to all holy relationships, I still think it is widely applicable. For instance, Helen and Bill's relationship is a classic case, in which two people joined in common purpose, which invited the Holy Spirit into their relationship. They then went through a "period of discomfort," and finally the Holy Spirit reached out through them to bring salvation to the world (in the form of *A Course in Miracles*).

In my own experience there is something very true about how the Course characterizes the holy relationship. A great deal of the focus of my life has been joining with others in common purpose. As with Helen and Bill, this invariably seems to invite some powerful Presence into our midst, an event which is inevitably followed by a period in which we are at each other's throats. Having been involved for many years in a small spiritual community, and having been led into life-long spiritually-based joinings with individuals, I feel I have some experience with this phenomenon, at least in its beginning stages. I am truly amazed at how accurately the Course seems to describe what we have gone through, and how insightful—and challenging—its suggestions are for change.

There is great power in what the Course is saying about holy relationships. I hope the second part of this book will help you to catch its vision and put it into practice.

~1~
A Common Purpose

What is a holy relationship?

We defined a special relationship as one in which I try to have a special interaction with a special person so that I can feel more special. In other words, I am simply using you so that I can achieve the goal of specialness. A holy relationship is truly different. It is one in which you and I have joined in a truly common goal and are journeying together toward that goal. In this way we have invited the goal of holiness into the relationship, so that *together* we can reach holiness.

The holy relationship, then, is a paradoxical creature. Because it is still journeying toward the goal of holiness it is still fraught with patterns of specialness. Yet it is holy because it has chosen the goal of holiness, because that goal has entered the relationship, and because the relationship will eventually reach that goal. This means that the relationship on some inner level is truly holy, but on the outer level may (and probably will) be still brimming with ego.

This also means that there is considerable subtlety and complexity around the term "holy relationship" in the Course. There are three somewhat distinct senses in which the term is used.

The first sense is the main one I will follow in this book. In this first sense, a holy relationship is a relationship which is in process toward holiness. As such, it is a *process.* The Course makes this abundantly clear in such passages as the following:

> In all its aspects, as it begins, develops and becomes accomplished, it represents the reversal of the unholy relationship (T-17.V.2:4).

> As this [beginning] change develops and is finally accomplished, it grows increasingly beneficent and joyous (T-17.V.5:3).

The holy relationship *begins, develops* and becomes *accomplished.* In this sense, it is clearly a process, an evolving thing that is growing toward the goal of holiness.

The second sense of the term is that the holy relationship is a *fully realized* holy relationship, one that has "become accomplished," that has reached its goal. This sense seems to predominate in the Manual and *Psychotherapy* pamphlet, from which the following passages are drawn:

> Each teaching-learning situation involves a different relationship at the beginning, although the ultimate goal is always the same; to make of the relationship a holy relationship, in which both can look upon the Son of God as sinless (M-3.1:2).

> This, however, needs the help of a very advanced therapist, capable of joining with the patient in a holy relationship in which all sense of separation finally is overcome (P-2.VII.3:6).

The third, and most subtle, sense of the term is that the holy relationship is that unconscious dimension of the relationship that is *already* fully realized, already holy, even while the conscious dimension is still in process (as in the first sense of the term). As we will discuss later, when two people join they allow the goal of holiness to enter the relationship, and this goal heals the relationship at an unconscious level. Now they have two relationships, you could say: their conscious interaction, still rife with specialness, and an inner dimension in which they are wholly joined, completely holy. We can see this use of the term when the Course breaks into praise of the relationship, saying things about it that are clearly not true on a conscious level, not yet at least:

> From your holy relationship truth proclaims the truth, and love looks on itself. Salvation flows from deep within the home you offered to my Father and to me. And we are there together, in the quiet communion in which the Father and the Son are joined. O come ye faithful to the holy union of the Father and the Son in you! (T-19.IV(B).7:1-4)

> Your relationship with your brother has been uprooted

from the world of shadows, and its unholy purpose has been safely brought through the barriers of guilt, washed with forgiveness, and set shining and firmly rooted in the world of light. From there it calls to you to follow the course it took, lifted high above the darkness and gently placed before the gates of Heaven (T-18.IX.13:1-2).

Notice that in both of the above passages, the holy relationship is said to be in a place of perfect holiness and we are assumed to be in a *different* place, for we are called to leave where we are and come join it where it is.

So we have three senses of the term "holy relationship":

1. A relationship that has allowed the goal of holiness to enter and is journeying toward that goal.

2. A relationship that has achieved the goal of holiness.

3. The unconscious dimension of number 1, the deep place in which the goal of holiness has already been fully realized.

Though I will mainly stick to the first sense, it will help to keep all three in mind as we read the Course and as we read the rest of this book.

Separate interests

As we all know, relationships in this world are generally pretty discouraging. We see the same sad patterns displayed in relationships between friends, romantic partners, spouses, children and parents, ethnic groups, nations, and even species. Stepping back and looking at these patterns, perhaps the primary thing we can say is that most of these relationships are illusions. They are not only illusions of love, as we said in Part I, they are illusions of *relationship*. They are not really relationships at all. For a relationship is a togetherness, a joining, a union of some sort. And what we find in this world is a profound aloneness even within supposed relationship, a deep divisiveness within apparent unity. As the Course says:

There is no order in relationships. They either are or not. An unholy relationship is no relationship. It is a state of isolation, which seems to be what it is not. No more than that (T-20.VI.8:1-5).

A passage we quoted in Part I is relevant again here:

And so they wander through a world of strangers, unlike themselves, living with their bodies perhaps under a common roof that shelters neither; in the same room and yet a world apart (T-22.IN.2:8).

We all know that when push comes to shove, as happens so frequently, everyone is primarily out for themselves. In essence, then, we are all playing the charade of togetherness while in truth remaining by ourselves. Apparently, our yearning for union has not overpowered our addiction to isolation.

Why are our relationships such shams, such illusions of togetherness? The Course has many explanations for this, many of which we discussed in Part I. Perhaps the most relevant to our current discussion is the idea that our relationships are knit "together" by separate goals, that I am in the relationship to satisfy my ends and you are in it to satisfy yours.

At the base of every relationship is its purpose. All relationships are brought together by an apparently common goal (the Course uses "goal" and "purpose" completely interchangeably). We come together because we want to do something together: run a business, raise a family, have fun, rebel against authority, experience love. We want to work together to reach some state or condition, some goal. And while we operate in joint pursuit of our successful business, or happy family, or good time, or loving experience, we seem to be really together. Yet are we? As we saw in our discussion of special relationships, this togetherness is usually a disguise, for when one of us stops holding up our end of the bargain, the disguise comes off and it becomes clear just how separate we really were.

We were not really holding a common goal. We simply found a common outer form that can coincidentally satisfy our separate interests. One can tell that our interests are still separate, for we each want that outer form for different reasons. I want our business to be successful because that brings me money and ego-gratification. You want our business to succeed because it brings *you* money and ego-gratification. I am in it for my ego and you are in it for your ego.

This idea of separate interests goes to the heart of the human condition. Separate interests does not mean being interested in different things. "Interest" here means "welfare" or "benefit." Separate interests is the idea that we do not benefit as one, that what benefits you does not benefit me. When you gain, I lose. If you get that food, I go hungry. If you get that mate, I am out in the cold. And since, in my eyes, I *must* gain, you must lose.

The relationship between interests and goals is quite simple. Goals are the things that we believe will serve our interests. We set a goal when we think that reaching or achieving that goal will benefit us, will be in our best interests. Hence, if you and I think we have separate interests, then my goals will serve my interests and yours will serve yours. Separate interests lead to competing goals. And competing goals lead to war, enmity, as this passage from *The Song of Prayer* states:

> Enemies do not share a goal. It is in this their enmity is kept. Their separate wishes are their arsenals; their fortresses in hate (S-1.IV.1:4-6).

Just what kind of goals do we choose when we believe that our interests are separate? Material goals, of course. We want to possess outer things; but not just outer objects like money and clothes. We want to possess desired situations and events. We want people to behave toward us in a certain way. We want the outer world to be arranged in a way that we think serves our interests. Yet these outer goals are merely means to our real end: specialness. This is our goal of goals. We want the outer world to arrange itself in certain ways because those ways send us the tangible message, "you are special." This is the goal that defines the special relationship as what it is. Remember our definition from Part I? A special relationship is one in which I try to have a special or exclusive interaction with a special person *so that I can feel more special*. That specialness is the whole purpose of the relationship.

In a special relationship, then, we have two separate goals. My goal is for me to feel more special. Your goal is for *you* to. Perhaps we can find a single form that accommodates both of our separate goals. This may mask the underlying enmity, but it does not eradicate it. Sooner or later that hidden enmity must come forth. Therefore, even while the mask is in place, we are not really friends. We are enemies who, while remaining enemies, have temporarily laid down our weapons, because for the moment we have agreed on a single situation that furthers our separate interests. We have simply found the *form* of relationship within the *content* of isolation.

> In dreams, no two can share the same intent. To each, the hero of the dream is different; the outcome wanted not the same for both....compromise alone a dream can bring. Sometimes it takes the form of union, but only the form....Minds cannot unite in dreams. They merely bargain (W-pI.185.3:3-4,4:1-2,4-5).

Separate interests is a central idea in the ego's system. The Course, in fact, calls this idea the only mistake there is: "For there is but one mistake; the whole idea that loss is possible, and could result in gain for anyone" (T-26.II.2:5). Conversely, the notion of common interests is pivotal in the Course's thought system. Common interests mean that we gain or lose together. We both gain or we both lose. The following two passages mention the idea of separate interests and affirm the reality of common interests:

> By this [fourth law of chaos], another's loss becomes your gain, and thus it fails to recognize that you can never take away save from yourself (T-23.II.9:4).

> Next, if you choose to take a thing away from someone else, you will have nothing left. This is because, when you deny his right to everything, you have denied your own....Who seeks to take away has been deceived by the illusion loss can offer gain. Yet loss must offer loss, and nothing more (W-pI.133.7).

At the base of almost every "friendly" relationship in this world are separate goals that have simply found a common form. What do we do with these relationships? Given the falsehood at their very foundation, must we not just throw them away on our search for God, as so many have done? The Course tells us over and over that the Holy Spirit has another way. He does not want us to discard our unholy relationships. He wants to transform them into holy relationships. But how?

The choice to see common interests

Given what we have just reviewed, we can appreciate the Course's claim that something of immense significance occurs when someone, even for a brief moment, breaks out of the mold of separate interests and sees just one other person as having the same interests. In that moment, says the Course, lies contained in seed-form the entire transcendence of the ego. In that moment the person's whole direction and destiny are changed. For, whether this person knows it or not, she has invited God into her mind and has signed a contract with God, agreeing from now on to devote her life to the salvation of all living things. Note these two significant passages from the Course material:

> A teacher of God is anyone who chooses to be one. His qualifications consist solely in this; somehow, somewhere he has made a deliberate choice in which he did not see his interests as apart from someone else's. Once he has done that, his road is established and his direction sure. A light has entered the darkness. It may be a single light, but that is enough. He has entered an agreement with God even if he does not yet believe in God. He has become a bringer of salvation. He has become a teacher of God (M-1.1).

> The unhealed healer may be arrogant, selfish, unconcerned, and actually dishonest. He may be uninterested in healing as his major goal. Yet something happened to him, however slight it may have been, when he chose to be a healer, however misguided the direction he may have chosen. That "something" is enough. Sooner or later that something will rise and grow... (P-3.II.3:2-6).

Joining in common purpose

This perception of common interests is the tool the Holy Spirit uses to transform our unholy relationships into holy ones. For if something of great significance happens when one person chooses to see common interests, imagine what happens when two people see the same interests in each other! Just as one person seeing common interests establishes him as a teacher of God, so two people seeing common interests establishes their relationship as holy. This perception of common interests is made possible by the sharing of a single common goal or purpose.

A common goal: this is what sparks the holy relationship. If we consider for a moment the implications of having a truly common purpose, we can see why this is so. First, let's gain some appreciation for the importance of a goal, a purpose.

A goal determines functioning and guides effort. When you choose a goal you automatically determine all of your activity, because your activity now will simply be an act of seeking your chosen goal. If you find that your activity is not a seeking of your goal, it is only because you have chosen other goals and are seeking *them.* So your goals determine all of your functioning and therefore determine your function as you see it.

> What is the purpose? Whatever it is, it will direct your efforts automatically. When you make a decision of purpose, then, you have made a decision about your future effort; a decision that will remain in effect unless you change your mind (T-4.V.6:9-11).

A goal determines experience by defining what things mean. When you really set a goal you will automatically see everything as a means to it. This is the meaning you will assign everything. This is easy to see in the case of someone who has really set a single, all-encompassing goal. Think, for instance, of a young entrepreneur who is consumed with the thought of making money. He will see everything—every situation, every event and even every person—as a potential means to his goal. That, to him, will be what everything is for. That will be what everything means to him. And that will determine how he experiences everything. If those things serve his goal well, he will like them. If they do not, he will be upset with them.

> And each one [each dream, each earthly experience] represents some function that you have assigned; some goal which an event, or body, or a thing *should* represent, and *should* achieve for you. If it succeeds you think you like the dream. If it should fail you think the dream is sad (T-29.IV.4:8-10).

So setting a goal determines the meaning you give things (because you will see everything as means to your goal), and the meaning you give things determines your experience of them.

A goal is all-determining for us. Based on the above two points a goal determines both our *expression*—what we do—and our *experience*—what we feel. And between these two is everything. Our expression and our experience constitute the whole of our earthly existence. What determines those two things is all-determining for us.

~ ~ ~

Now based on the above points, what is the significance of sharing a goal? If a goal determines the whole of our earthly existence, both our expression and our experience, then *sharing a goal is sharing everything*. If you and I share the same purpose, we will have the same function. We will direct our efforts in the same direction. Our activities will be guided by the same intent. We will see everything as a means to the same end. We will see the same meaning in everything. We will evaluate all outcomes by the same standard. We will have the same experience of things. And if we have the same experience, then we must be gaining or losing together. Our interests must be the same, such that my welfare is your welfare, my benefit is yours.

In short, sharing a common goal gives us the experience of being one. Oneness of purpose yields oneness of mind. This, says the Course, is the law of purpose:

Only a purpose unifies, and those who share a purpose have a mind as one (T-23.IV.7:4).

What shares a common purpose is the same. This is the law of purpose, which unites all those who share in it within itself (T-27.VI.1:5-6).

In other words, sharing a common goal reverses the entire ladder of the ego's relationships. That ladder started with separateness, isolation, and led to the perception of difference and competing interests. Sharing a common purpose leads to the perception of common interests and sameness, which replaces isolation with togetherness. As the Course says, "a single function...would mean a shared identity..." (T-27.II.11:6). And since isolation is the core of the ego, sharing a common purpose is an actual, practical step outside of the ego. It is the realization of oneness on a very practical level in this world.

Examples of a common purpose

Let us look at a couple of examples of finding a common goal. The first involves the scribes of the Course, Helen Schucman and Bill Thetford. As mentioned in the Introduction to Part II, their holy relationship was both the catalyst for the Course and its initial reason for being. They spent about seven years after they met in a relationship which involved a great deal of conflict and pain, set within a working environment that was also torn with conflict. Then, one day, as Helen tells it, she and Bill were talking and...

> [Bill] delivered a speech....He had been thinking things over and had concluded we were using the wrong approach. "There must," he said, "be another way...." It was a long speech for Bill, and he spoke with unaccustomed emphasis. There was no doubt that he meant what he said. When it was over he waited for my response in obvious discomfort. Whatever reaction he may have expected, it was certainly not the one he got. I jumped up, told Bill with genuine conviction that he was perfectly right, and said I would join in the new approach with him (*Absence from Felicity*, Kenneth Wapnick, p. 93, 94).

To translate this into the terms we have just been using, Helen and Bill joined in a common purpose. This purpose, it seems, was to find and demonstrate a more loving, constructive, cooperative way of relating.

This moment of joining, in which a unified purpose enters a relationship dominated by divisiveness, is an example of what the Course calls a holy instant. In the holy instant we disconnect from the past and our habitual frame of reference, and open ourselves up to a new experience, a new way of looking at things.

Another example of finding a common goal comes from the *Psychotherapy* pamphlet, dictated through Helen after the Course's completion. Part of this pamphlet's unique vision of psychotherapy is that what makes therapy successful is not so much what the therapist tells the patient; the success of therapy lies in establishing a holy relationship between therapist and client. And, since doing so requires them to reach a common goal, the reaching of that goal is a major theme in the pamphlet.

We are told that at first therapist and patient have divided goals. The patient enters therapy with the goal that he will learn how to feel better without changing his self-concept—the source of his suffering—in any way. The therapist, on the other hand, has the agenda of changing the patient "in some way that he believes is real" (P-2.IN.4:1). In other words, the therapist wants to change the patient; the patient wants to resist change. They are at cross purposes. Their goals are divided.

> The task of therapy is one of reconciling these differences. Hopefully, both will learn to give up their original goals, for it is only in relationships that salvation can be found. At the beginning, it is inevitable that patients and therapists alike accept unrealistic goals not completely free of magical overtones. They are finally given up in the minds of both (P-2.IN.4:2-5).

I find this to be a very significant passage. First, it tells us that the whole task of therapy is one of reconciling their divergent goals. For once their goals are united, healing flows automatically. In other words, it is not what the therapist does to the patient, or what the patient allows to be done to himself, *"for it is only in relationships that salvation can be found."* Only in joining together with someone else will we be healed, "for no one will find sanity alone" (P-2.II.5:7). Along these lines, the following is perhaps the Course's best description of the holy relationship:

> What must the therapist do to bring healing about? Only one thing; the same requirement salvation asks of everyone. Each one must share one goal with someone else, and in so doing lose all sense of separate interests. Only by doing this is it possible to transcend the narrow boundaries the ego would impose upon the self. Only by doing this can teacher and pupil, therapist and patient, you and I, accept Atonement and learn to give it as it was received (P-2.II.8).

So what must be the common purpose of therapist and patient?

This is not spelled out, but it is implied clearly enough. Patient and therapist must join together in the real function of therapy, in the goal of changing not who the patient *really* is, but who the patient *thinks* he is. In experiencing the fulfillment of this goal together, both the patient and the therapist will find their healing.

How do we apply this to our own lives? What would a common purpose really look like? We are told in the *Psychotherapy* pamphlet that any purpose is acceptable, as long as it is one that can truly be shared. "It does not matter what their purpose is, but they must share it wholly to succeed" (P-2.II.6:6). For instance, it need have no conscious or overt reference to God.

Whether or not any particular goal is truly shared comes down to the answer to this question: Is the goal that I am pursuing something that only I can possess, or something that I and my partner can actually possess together? A shared goal means that when we reach the goal, we can share it.

If my goal is something external it cannot truly be shared. When you and I have made money together, it is not actually shared. I own half and you own half. More importantly, behind all material goals lies the goal of specialness, and specialness cannot be shared. By nature, specialness is exclusive. It is about me. Even when it looks collective—our superior family, my championship team, our exalted country—it still comes down to how my family, team or country enhances my specialness. Just as with the money, I own my *share* of that specialness.

The only goal that allows for true joining is the realization of an abstract idea. For, as the Course points out again and again, ideas can be truly shared. If our goal is to realize the same idea, we can do that together. We can both experience the same idea at the same time. We do not experience our part of it, our share. We both experience all of the idea. This is what Helen and Bill did in joining together in search of a better way. Even the therapist and patient, who join together for the sake of the patient, are doing this, for the patient's real Identity is an idea, one that far transcends their individual egos.

Therefore, only a goal that is truly holy can be shared. And conversely, if a goal has been truly shared, it must be holy.

> Whatever resolutions patient and therapist reach in connection with their own divergent goals, they cannot become completely reconciled as one until they join with His. Only then is all conflict over... (P-2.I.3:6-7).

It is impossible to share a goal not blessed by Christ, for what is unseen through His eyes is too fragmented to be meaningful (P-2.II.6:7).

I think that the process of reconciling divergent goals and finding a truly common purpose will be different in each relationship. I think that in each relationship there is a common purpose already sleeping within it, waiting to be uncovered, one that uniquely fits that relationship. And I am sure that the process of uncovering this purpose will always be different. In some relationships it may need to be a very overt and conscious search which will even result in a written purpose, while in others the goal may come to light and become shared without being spoken, or even without the people involved being able to put their finger on what exactly the purpose is.

And while I am sure that the people involved can benefit from applying themselves to finding this purpose, this must be done sensitively, for it simply cannot be forced. For one, it must be truly mutual. Joining in this goal must come freely and sincerely from the heart of each person. True, it does take two, but one person forcing the other is simply not going to work. The best that each person can do is to diligently work on their own end, on uncovering their own blocks to joining. Another reason that it cannot be forced is that the moment of joining is a moment of grace. It is arranged by Heaven, not by us. Forcing it is like saying, "On such-and-such a day, at 2:38 PM, I will have an experience of Divine grace." All we can do is give up our own resistance to oneness and wait for the other person and the Holy Spirit to respond. According to the Course, if we make our choice for oneness, the Holy Spirit will respond immediately, and it will be only a matter of time before the other person will respond, too.

Trying to force someone to share a common purpose with you can be a great temptation. It is so easy for the ego to latch onto this idea of the holy relationship and try to make it happen, and then perhaps cut off the relationship if it does not. This is a temptation to really watch out for. It can look holy, but of course it is just attack in the name of holiness, another version of that traditional favorite of going to war in the name of God.

~*2*~
The Holy Relationship is Mutual, not Individual

erhaps the most pervasive misconception about the holy relationship is the idea that it exists only in the mind of the individual, that my relationship with you is holy when it is holy in my mind, regardless of how you hold the relationship in your mind. In other words, our relationship can be holy if I forgive you, but you still hate me; or if I see common interests, but you only see separate goals.

In seeing the holy relationship as mutual I am aware that I am in the distinct minority (along with Allen Watson, my teaching partner at The Circle of Atonement). Some time ago I was told by an author of Course-based material that he had polled five prominent Course teachers on this topic. Despite all their other differences, these teachers had all agreed that a relationship was holy if only one person forgave. In addition to a majority of Course teachers, I would bet that a majority of students holds this same view.

Though we Course students tend to shy away from "issues" and would like to affirm that every possible point of view is equally right, this is an issue we cannot dodge. What is really at stake is the nature of a holy relationship. One position says that a relationship is holy at those moments when one of the two people is forgiving the other. The other position (my own) says that a holy relationship is a process in which two people have an initial joining in a common goal and then go through a lengthy process of jointly realizing that goal. These two positions are so far removed that practically the only thing they have in common is the term "holy relationship." In a discussion of holy relationships, the issue of what a holy relationship is, is fundamental. We cannot dodge it.

Because this is such an important topic, I would like to devote some space to this. What follows are my reasons for believing that when the Course talks about a holy relationship, it is referring to a very distinct phenomenon in which two people have mutually joined in a common goal and are on a journey of jointly realizing that goal.

Ten reasons for the mutuality of the holy relationship

1. The Course always speaks of the holy relationship as involving two people.

The Course is very consistent in talking about the holy relationship using the language of "two-ness." Every time the Course mentions a holy relationship, the passage either implies or openly states that it involves two. Here are just a few of the passages where this can be seen easily:

> You undertook, together, to invite the Holy Spirit into your relationship. *He could not have entered otherwise* (T-17.V.11:1-2; emphasis mine).

> In your newness, remember that you and your brother have started again, *together.* And take his hand, to walk together along a road far more familiar than you now believe (T-17.V.9:3-4).

> Time has been readjusted to help us do, together, what your separate pasts would hinder. You have gone past fear, for no two minds can join in the desire for love without love's joining them (T-18.III.7:6-7).

> You and your brother are coming home together, after a long and meaningless journey that you undertook apart, and that led nowhere. You have found your brother, and you will light each other's ways (T-18.III.8:5-6).

> You whose hand is joined with your brother's have begun to reach beyond the body, but not outside yourself, to reach your shared Identity together (T-18.VI.10:2).

> A holy relationship is a means of saving time. One instant

spent together restores the universe to both of you....Time has been saved for you because you and your brother are together (T-18.VII.5:2-3, 6:3).

And you will not be able to give love welcome separately. You could no more know God alone than He knows you without your brother. But together you could no more be unaware of love than love could know you not... (T-18.VIII.12:3-5; emphasis mine).

The ark of peace is entered two by two, yet the beginning of another world goes with them. Each holy relationship must enter here... (T-20.IV.6:5-6).

In this world, God's Son comes closest to himself in a holy relationship....Two voices raised together call to the hearts of everyone, to let them beat as one (T-20.V.1:1, 2:3).

Rejoice whom God hath joined have come together and need no longer look on sin apart. No two can look on sin together, for they could never see it in the same place and time (T-22.IN.1:2-3).

A holy relationship starts from a different premise. *Each one* has looked within and seen no lack (T-22.IN.3:1-2; emphasis mine).

What, then, has joined them? Reason will tell you that they must have seen each other through a vision not of the body....Rather, *in each* the other saw a perfect shelter where his Self could be reborn in safety and in peace (T-22.I.9:8; emphasis mine).

Such is the function of a holy relationship; to receive together and give as you received (T-22.IV.7:4).

Yet if pupil and teacher join in sharing one goal, God will enter into their relationship... (P-2.II.5:3).

God's Teacher speaks to any two who join together for learning purposes. The relationship is holy because of that purpose (M-2.5:3-4).

Note that in some of these quotes the mutuality is explicitly said to be necessary to the relationship's holiness. The first quote says that unless you invited the Holy Spirit together He could not have entered. The seventh one says that you cannot welcome love separately, without your brother. The last one says that the relationship is holy because two have joined in a holy purpose. We will return to this idea in point 3.

2. The Course never once says that a holy relationship takes only one.

I will venture to say that this is not my opinion, but a fact. There just is not anywhere in the Course that speaks of the holy relationship needing only one person. I have spent many years looking for such a reference in the Course. I have made this claim in many places, both in writing and in person, to many students and teachers. Neither I nor anyone else has been able to supply me with a place in the Course that says a relationship is holy when one person forgives another.

There are two passages that people give me the most often. One is in "The Happy Dream," in Chapter 18, where the Course says, "Whoever is saner at the time" (7:1) should accept a holy instant for both people. First, note this does not say "whoever is saner at the time should make the relationship holy." Second and more pertinent, this passage openly assumes a holy relationship has already been established. It begins (in 6:1) by saying, "When you feel the holiness of your relationship is threatened by anything...." It goes on to say (see 6:3-7) that *because* your relationship is holy one of you can ask for a holy instant for both. In other words, this well-known passage actually means, "*Because* your relationship has been made holy, when any disturbance comes up, whoever is saner at the time can accept a holy instant for both of you."

The other passage is the source of the oft-quoted idea that it takes two to separate and one to heal:

No mind is sick until another mind agrees that they are separate. And thus it is their joint decision to be sick. If you withhold agreement and accept the part you play in making sickness real, the other mind cannot project its guilt without your aid in letting it perceive itself as separate and apart from you (T-28.III.2:1-3).

So, the reasoning goes, if it takes only one to heal, then it takes only one to heal a relationship, and thus it takes only one to make a relationship holy. Let's look at this passage. First, we will notice that it is talking about the healing of sickness, not about a holy relationship. Second, we should also note that it speaks about the power of *joint* decision, of *two* minds agreeing, and the ability of one person to influence that joint decision. In essence, it says that in order to believe in sickness, another person needs the power of my agreement. If I withdraw agreement and see him as healed, he will not be able to hang onto his belief in sickness, which means he will have to agree with me. He will eventually have to *join* my decision. The paragraph ends by saying, "Healing is the effect of minds that join, while sickness comes from minds that separate" (T-28.III.2:6). In other words, either both minds will agree to be separate, or both minds will (eventually) agree to be joined. And, as it says elsewhere in the Course, when both agree to be joined, the relationship is holy.

I am completely satisfied that the Course contains no passage that says the holy relationship takes only one.

3. The Course makes two-ness inherent to the meaning and significance of the holy relationship and to every stage in its progression.

This is probably the most important point. The whole meaning of the holy relationship is the transcending of separateness through the joint experience of oneness. As the Course puts it, our core disease is separation. This separation is experienced between ourselves and everything else, including God. Yet it is in our relationships with other people that we can heal it. The holy relationship is the actual overcoming of separation. It is the transcendence of isolation and its replacement with union. This transcendence of "the narrow boundaries the ego would impose upon the self" (P-2.II.8:5), is the whole point of salvation. Thus, when two seemingly separate parts meet and realize their oneness, the whole of salvation is contained in that one act.

The pivotal importance of replacing the ego's isolation with authentic interpersonal union is underscored in many ways in the Course. First, we must remember that the writing of the Course was sparked by Helen and Bill transcending their separate interests and establishing a truly mutual purpose, and that initially the Course's reason for being was to help them attain this purpose together. Second, there are two places in the Course which describe in detail the contrast between the special and holy relationship ("The Temple of the Holy Spirit," in Chapter 20 and the Introduction to Chapter 22). In both of these places the primary contrast between special and holy relationships is between *separateness* and *togetherness, isolation* and *union*. Finally, there are particular passages that state very clearly the central importance of the replacement of isolation with union. For instance,

> Salvation must reverse the mad belief in separate thoughts and separate bodies, which lead separate lives and go their separate ways. One function shared by separate minds unites them in one purpose... (W-pI.100.1:2-3).

> When two minds join as one and share one idea equally, the first link in the awareness of the Sonship as one has been made (T-16.II.4:3).

Let's look closely at this second passage. If we start from the end of it, we see it sets out a final goal: "the awareness of the Sonship as one." This refers to the goal of the entire Sonship, every living mind, realizing its oneness, awakening as one Self. The final goal is that we all together realize our unity as the single Son of God. The first step to this goal, according to this passage, is for just two minds to join and share one idea equally, which, of course, is a reference to a holy relationship. Do you see the logic of this? If the final goal is for everyone to realize their oneness, the first step towards that goal is for just two to realize their oneness. Actually, the term is "first *link*." Before we all can link up together in oneness there must be the *first* link, where just two link up.

The holy relationship, then, is the harbinger of the heavenly state, the "herald of eternity," as it is put in Chapter 20, Section V. We all know that the heavenly state is mutual, communal. And the holy relationship, being a first step in that direction, is mutual as well. It is a miniature example of the all-encompassing mutuality of Heaven.

Throughout the rest of this book we will be tracking the stages the holy relationship goes through on the way to its goal. I have included one way of listing those stages in a chart. Next to each stage is an explanation of what the Course says about this stage (condensed from actual passages from

CHART

The Initiation of a Holy Relationship	Two minds, at least for an instant, join in sharing a single purpose. *Mutuality.*
The Initial Period of Discomfort	Both individuals are afraid that the *relationship* (as a *two-some*) will never reach its goal. *Assumes mutuality.*
Faith in the Goal	Both individuals must try to strengthen their faith in the accomplishment of the goal. *Assumes mutuality.*
Forgiveness	Each one must forgive the other so that both forgive and save each other. *Assumes mutuality.*
Utilizing Oneness	Because what one thinks the other will experience, either one can save the other. They should join in joint holy instants. From the standpoint of their oneness they can see that the ego is illusion. *Mutuality.*
Joint Special Function	The two are given a joint special function, a way of together serving the salvation of all minds. *Mutuality.*
Final Goal	The two lose sight of all separateness between them, and serve the goal of the entire Sonship losing sight of all separateness between its parts. *Mutuality.*

the Course) and how this assumes that the holy relationship is mutual, takes two.

If the above is correct, and we then read the term "holy relationship" as, "any relationship in which one person has forgiven the other," then we miss the entire point of the term. It would be like hearing the word "wedding" and thinking, "Oh, that's when one person shows up at the altar."

4. The Course says what happens when only one person does his or her part.

As we have discussed, the Course says what happens when two people see their interests as the same (by joining in the same goal): A holy relationship is established. Significantly, the Course also says what happens when one personal alone does this. Something equally significant but different happens: He becomes a teacher of God.

In fact, both of these things are said in the same discussion in the Manual. We already quoted from Section 1 of the Manual, which says that when you make one choice to see one other person's interests as not apart from yours, you become a teacher of God. The next section (which continues the discussion of the teacher of God's journey) tells us the results of this. Your pupils begin to look for you, finally coming to the right place at the right time to meet you. You and they then join in the common purpose of learning the same course, and this makes the relationship holy. "The relationship is holy because of that purpose..." (M-2.5:4).

When you alone see common interests you become a teacher of God. When you establish a common goal with someone else you begin a holy relationship.

5. The mutuality of the holy relationship goes beyond the Text discussions and so is not simply an artifact of Helen and Bill's relationship.

I have heard it said that the Text talks so clearly about two people joining because it was speaking personally to Helen and Bill's relationship, and they just happened to have a relationship in which two people consciously joined. This mutual joining, it is claimed, is not an inherent part of the holy relationship, but was merely part of the *particular* holy relationship the Course was speaking to.

We have really already ruled this out in point #3 above, where we said the Course makes mutuality central to the meaning of the holy relationship. However, we can rule this idea out in an additional way. For only the Text discussions of the holy relationship were speaking directly to Helen and Bill's relationship. The holy relationship discussions in the Manual and in the *Psychotherapy* pamphlet were not. The Manual was speaking to any relationship between a teacher and pupil. The *Psychotherapy* pamphlet was speaking to any relationship between a therapist and patient. These places talk about the holy relationship in the same way as the Text, as a mutual joining in a common goal.

6. The Course discussions of the holy relationship are grounded in specific examples in which the two-ness is totally unambiguous.

This takes off from the previous point. The Text was speaking to Helen and Bill, whom we know both joined in the search for "a better way."

The Manual speaks of a teacher and pupil who physically meet at the right time and place (M-2.4:4) and mutually join in learning the same course (M-2.5:7).

The *Psychotherapy* pamphlet speaks of a therapist and patient who sit down together for therapy sessions and initially hold divergent goals, but who eventually reconcile those goals and join together in the Holy Spirit's goal (see P-2.IN.4, 2.I.3:6-7).

The Song of Prayer speaks of two people who have realized they share a goal and who as an expression of that realization are sitting down and praying together for the same things, the same goal (see S-1.IV.1-3).

As I said in the Introduction to Part II, these four discussions of the holy relationship are the only ones in the Course material. Therefore, *all* of the Course's discussions of the holy relationship are organized around and speak of relationships that are unambiguously mutual. Where is the evidence for the relationship made holy by just one person?

7. The idea of salvation depending on a mutual joining is not in conflict with the Course's basic thought system.

The final four points will deal with the main objection to the holy relationship as a mutual joining: It can't take two. In my experience, when people object to the holy relationship as a mutual joining, it is not based on actual passages from the Course (we have seen there are no such passages). It is based simply on the idea that the holy relationship *can't* be that way—

for various reasons.

The first reason it can't be that way is that, in this view, the Course clearly teaches that my salvation depends solely on my individual act of accepting the Atonement for myself. Early in the Text we are told, *"The sole responsibility of the miracle worker is to accept the Atonement for himself"* (T-2.V.5:1). Yet this line does not mean what students often think it means. It does not speak of the sole responsibility of the "Course student," but of the *"miracle worker"*—one who works miracles, who extends miracles to a *miracle receiver*. Just a few sentences before this famous line we are told that the "miracle worker" (3:5) must be in his right mind, however briefly, if he is going to restore the "miracle receiver" (3:2) to *his* right mind. In other words, this line really means, "The sole precondition for giving miracles to others is accepting the Atonement for yourself."

We might ask, then, where does the miracle *receiver's* salvation come from? Does it not in part come from someone else, from the miracle *worker*? Yes, of course it does. This idea that my salvation comes strictly from my individual choice, unaided by anyone else, does not reflect the Course. In many, many places the Course speaks of salvation as "a collaborative venture" (T-4.VI.8:2, 8.IV.4:8). The *Psychotherapy* pamphlet puts it starkly:

> Teacher and pupil, therapist and patient, are all insane or they would not be here. Together they can find a pathway out, for no one will find sanity alone (P-2.II.5:6-7).

The holy relationship as a mutual joining is not a contradiction of the Course's basic thought system, but an extension of it.

8. Thinking it takes two does not necessarily result in people abdicating responsibility for their own salvation.

Another reason why the holy relationship supposedly can't be mutual is that, if we think it is, we will abdicate our personal responsibility. We will get enmeshed in unhealthy co-dependency. We will go around forcing people to join with us. Or we will go crazy when our holy unions do not work out, since salvation is now impossible for us (I heard a true story in which this happened).

True, all of the above happens. Thinking that the holy relationship is mutual leads to excesses and abuses. But so does everything else in life, including the Course itself. To say that the idea must thereby be false is a classic case of throwing the baby out with the bathwater.

There is a way to realize that the other person plays a role in my salvation and still stay focused on my responsibility. The Course, in fact, teaches such a way. In a holy relationship, it says, we both are each other's saviors. We save each other by forgiving each other. I cannot make it back without your forgiveness, nor you without mine. Yet this does not mean that I should sit around and wait for you to save me, and resent you until you do. Rather, I set you free to save me by saving *you*, by forgiving *you*. "Be certain, if you do your part, he will do his, for he will join you where you stand" (T-28.IV.5:1). In a way, my forgiveness of you is the "on" switch that activates your role as my savior. Thus, if I want you to do your part, I should focus all my attention on doing *mine*.

Seen truly, then, the mutuality of the holy relationship is an incentive for me to exercise my responsibility, rather than a deterrent.

9. The idea that we cannot find a partner who will join with us is not supported by the Course.

A very common objection to the notion that the holy relationship is mutual is that I will not be able to find someone to join with me. If it takes two then it seems that my salvation hangs on the highly uncertain prospect of me finding someone who will join with me. Further, I definitely feel ready for such a person and they have not shown up. Therefore, I can conclude that either salvation is manifestly unfair, or it just does not work this way—it does not take two to make a relationship holy.

As reasonable as the above sounds, the Course directly refutes it. It says quite clearly that when you are *truly* ready to join, people will show up who are ready to join with you. Let us draw again on the first two sections in the Manual for Teachers. First, someone makes a deliberate choice in which he does not see his interests as separate from someone else's (M-1:2). This means that he is ready to join. This choice then sets off an internal signal in those who are ready to join with him (in this case, his pupils). They "begin to look for him as soon as he has answered the Call" (M-2.1:1). Finally, they come to the right place at the right time (M-2.4:4), meet him and join him in a common purpose, a holy relationship, in which all sense of difference and separateness ultimately disappears (M-2.5).

When we read this we may well think, "Yeah but what if it does not work? What if a signal gets crossed and the two never quite make it to the right place and time and thus never meet?" The Manual's answer is that it is absolutely *inevitable* that they meet. Why? To understand the answer we must grasp something of the Course's theory of time. In that theory, the first instant of the separation contained all of the long drama that would apparently play out over billions of years, including the final act of our return home. So in that first instant the separation began, was played out and ended. However, out of our attachment to the drama we decided to replay it in our minds, to watch the movie of what was already over. According to the Course, this is what we are doing right now. The scene before us has already happened. It is not really happening now. Our experience of it is merely us reviewing a memory, a memory that only seems real and present.

This means that if, in that ancient instant, I met the person who would join with me, then I will inevitably meet him or her now. The chances that this will not be are the same as the chances that Dorothy will not meet the Scarecrow the next time I watch *The Wizard of Oz*. Here is the passage from the Manual:

> And thus it is that pupil and teacher seem to come together in the present, finding each other *as if* they had not met before. The pupil comes at the right time to the right place. This is *inevitable,* because he made the right choice in that ancient instant *which he now relives* (M-2.4:3-5; emphasis mine).

Section 3 in the Manual makes the same point, just as directly:

> Therefore, the plan includes very specific contacts to be made for each teacher of God. There are no accidents in salvation. *Those who are to meet will meet, because together they have the potential for a holy relationship.* They are ready for each other (M-3.1:5-8; emphasis mine).

Lesson 185 in the Workbook is similarly clear on this idea.

> The mind which means that all it wants is peace must join with other minds, for that is how peace is obtained. And when the wish for peace is genuine, the means for finding it is given, in a form each mind that seeks for it in

honesty can understand (W-pI.185.6:1-2).

We could put these two sentences together to read thus, "To obtain peace you must join with other minds, and when you really want peace the other minds to join with are given you."

Thus, however reasonable our ideas to the contrary may seem, the Course itself is crystal clear that if we are ready for a holy relationship, we *will*, inevitably, without question, meet the people with whom we have a potential for a holy relationship.

10. The idea that we cannot rely on a partner to do his or her part is not supported by the Course.

Meeting this person, however, is only the beginning. Many of us have met someone who seemed the very embodiment of the promise of a holy relationship, only to have our hopes dashed as the relationship proceeded. As a result it can seem as if no one will really carry through and do their part. Surely, we conclude, the Course cannot really be resting our salvation on such unreliable people.

According to the Course, this thought is a major egoic defense on our part against the holy relationship, a defense the Course calls lack of faith in our brother. We will discuss this more fully in Chapter 4. What we can say here, however, is that the Course thinks differently:

> The goal establishes the fact that everyone involved in it
> will play his part in its accomplishment. This is inevitable.
> No one will fail in anything (T-17.VI.6:5-7).

To say that the holy relationship cannot be mutual because we cannot count on other people is the ego's reasoning, not the Course's. As we will see in Chapter 4, our lack of faith in our brother is what blocks the holy relationship from fulfilling its purpose. How natural, then, that this same faithlessness would block us from understanding what the holy relationship is. In this case, as perhaps in other cases, our objections to the holy relationship being a mutual joining are also our objections to joining itself.

~ ~ ~

In my mind the preceding ten points make an exceedingly strong case. The case is so strong simply because the Course itself is unambiguous on this matter.

Yet this point also needs to be carefully qualified. For regardless of whether we are in a special relationship or a holy relationship (as I am defining it here), our job is the *same*. Whatever relationship we are in, our job is to forgive, to see past the body and its "sins" to the Christ within the other person. To this fundamental exercise the issue of whether or not that person has chosen to join with us is irrelevant. It can be just as hard or harder to forgive when someone has joined us on a common journey as when they have not.

In a special relationship we can not only forgive, we can even individually invite the Holy Spirit into the relationship:

> Sooner or later that something will rise and grow; a patient will touch his heart, and the therapist will silently ask him for help. He has himself found a therapist. *He has asked the Holy Spirit to enter the relationship and heal it.* He has accepted the Atonement for himself (P-3.II.3:6-9; emphasis mine).

> You can place any relationship under His care and be sure that it will not result in pain, if you offer Him your willingness to have it serve no need but His (T-15.V.5:4).

> Leave Him His function, for He will fulfill it if you but ask Him to enter your relationships, and bless them for you (T-16.I.7:9).

This third passage refers to using the following beautiful prayer to ask the Holy Spirit to enter a relationship, I prayer I highly recommend that we really use:

> *I am not alone, and I would not intrude the past upon my Guest.*
> *I have invited Him, and He is here.*
> *I need do nothing except not to interfere* (T-16.I.3:10-12).

The Course does not call this a holy relationship. Presumably, the relationship would not be made holy until both people together asked the Holy Spirit in (the Course says as much in T-17.V.11:1-2). However, when one person invites the Holy Spirit into the relationship in true sincerity, it is only a matter of time until the other one will also. Remember the line we quoted earlier, "Be certain, if you do your part, he will do his..." (T-28.IV.5:1).

Our job in the holy relationship is the same as our job in the special relationship, and for a very good reason: A holy relationship is still a special relationship in the process of shedding its specialness. As we said in Chapter 1, a holy relationship is one in which the goal of holiness has entered, a relationship that is on the way to that goal but has not yet reached it and so is still laden with patterns of specialness. So what I am calling a holy relationship could also be called a special relationship that has chosen to make the journey to holiness. This means that either way, special or holy, the lessons are the same. The lesson is always the overcoming of specialness through forgiveness.

The main difference between special and holy, then, is that a holy relationship is a more effective classroom, because another has joined with us. It is simply more useful. We all know that power lies in joining. I think there are very few of us who would not make quicker progress in any area, including the area of spiritual development, if someone else were really joined with us in that pursuit. This reminds me of one of the inner visions Helen had preceding the Course.

> I was crossing a bridge in very heavy traffic. I wanted to make a right turn, but I was in the wrong lane and another car was blocking my way. Both of us were crowded in, with cars in front and behind. The whole situation seemed to be one large traffic jam. There seemed to be no way I could make the turn, even though it was essential that I do so. "If I try to turn I'll crash into that car next to me," I thought, "and if he turns right I won't have time to follow before the gap will close and I'll be jammed in again." I kept trying to think up ways to make the turn, but all of them were inadequate and some disastrous. And then the solution came to me.
>
> "We'll both make it together," I thought, happily. "It won't be any trouble at all."
>
> And so I made the turn along with the man in the car

next to me. It was very easy. "It's funny I never thought of that before," I said to myself as the picture faded *(Journey Without Distance*, p. 45).

As in Helen's vision, making the turn with someone else is simply easier than making it alone. The holy relationship is the ideal classroom for learning how to turn off the ego's road onto a new path.

I have been through many discussions about holy relationships in which the main issue is figuring out which relationships qualify as holy. That term sounds so lovely that we want to be able to claim it, to pin it on particular relationships. It seems that most of our energy on this topic goes into deciding which relationships of ours merit this exalted title.

Yet, of course, such pursuit entirely misses the point of holy relationships. The point is not to claim the title. The point is to make use of the classroom. A relationship in which we truly share a common goal contains enormous potential for quick spiritual progress. As the *Psychotherapy* pamphlet says,

> Neither can do this alone, but when they join, the potentiality for transcending all limitations has been given them. Now the extent of their success depends on how much of this potentiality they are willing to use (P-2.III.2:3-4).

"The potentiality for transcending all limitations." This is a magnificent promise. Now we must simply be willing to use this potentiality. Therefore, I suggest that we funnel our energy into this, into tapping the potential of the holy relationship, and not spend so much time trying to figure out which relationships we can attach the label to.

~3~
Holiness Enters
the Relationship

*T*o recap: Two people whose relationship was formerly based on separate interests, have now reached a single common goal. On an appearance level, this event may not look like much. But on an inner, unconscious level, something happens that is so significant as to be earth-shaking, and, in the end, earth-dispelling. Because this significance is so much more than we would guess from viewing the outer appearance, much of the Course's discussion of the holy relationship aims at vividly describing this event that is invisible to our normal eyes.

A relationship that has just accepted a common goal will probably seem changed. And the moment in which the joining occurred will most likely seem like a significant moment. Yet the relationship will probably go on displaying roughly the same patterns as before. And the moment of joining may soon lose its vital importance in the eyes of the two people. They may even come to doubt that the joining really occurred. I am sure that this is not always the case. In my experience the moment of joining can feel more significant than anything that has ever happened. Yet even when this is true, the relationship will not instantly demonstrate real holiness. And the people involved will often come to doubt how authentic their experience was, or at least how much power it can hold against the forces of ego that seem intent on snuffing it out.

Yet, again, the Course tells us that we have no idea of the incomprehensible significance of what just happened: "You are so used to choosing among dreams you do not see that you have made, at last, the choice between the truth and all illusions" (T-18.II.8:6). Something happened in that moment of joining that the Course spends paragraph after paragraph trying to describe, returning to it again and again. Somehow, in that single moment of looking into each other's eyes and seeing the same interests and setting the same goal, the journey to God was over. In that moment we were saved. "Your perception was healed in the holy instant Heaven gave you....you who were sightless have been given vision, and you can see (T-19.III.10:4,6). "Condemn salvation not, for it has come to you" (T-17.V.10:6).

Yet, strangely, we have become so accustomed to the journey that we do not recognize the end of it, even though we are there.

> You have reached the end of an ancient journey, not realizing yet that it is over. You are still worn and tired, and the desert's dust still seems to cloud your eyes and keep you sightless. Yet He Whom you welcomed has come to you... (T-18.IX.13:1-3).

> Prisoners bound with heavy chains for years, starved and emaciated, weak and exhausted, and with eyes so long cast down in darkness they remember not the light, do not leap up in joy the instant they are made free. It takes a while for them to understand what freedom is. You groped but feebly in the dust and found your brother's hand, uncertain whether to let it go or to take hold on life so long forgotten. Strengthen your hold and raise your eyes unto your strong companion, in whom the meaning of your freedom lies. He seemed to be crucified beside you. And yet his holiness remained untouched and perfect, and with him beside you, you shall this day enter with him to Paradise, and know the peace of God (T-20.III.9).

Think about this: When you unite with another under a common goal something in you becomes enlightened in that moment. And from that time on, all you need do is realize that the journey is, in fact, over. You need only realize that you have crossed the finish line and stop running, sit down and enjoy your victory.

How can this be? It seems too easy to be true. What happened in that moment that the Course ascribes so much significance to?

The Holy Spirit enters the relationship

What happens is that by uniting in a common goal you invite the Holy Spirit and His goal into your relationship. You may not know that. You may think that you are together to save the whale. You may not even think there is a Holy Spirit. Yet the Holy Spirit does not really care about formal beliefs. What He cares about is the overcoming of the ego. The ego blocks Him out; joining—any kind of real joining—invites Him in. "If any two are joined, He must be there" (P-2.II.6:5).

And so, when Helen and Bill joined together to find "another way," to their surprise Helen began having visions of Jesus. It is not that he began knocking on the door of their relationship; he was already inside. He had, in fact, taken charge of the relationship and was now guiding it to its goal.

Similarly, when client and therapist join in seeking healing for the client's self-concept, by doing so, whether they know it or not, they have invited the Divine Healer into their midst. And this Healer will take the relationship under His wing and from that moment on shepherd it toward its goal.

Essentially, when two join in common purpose, by the mere fact of transcending the ego's isolation, they open a sluice through which comes pouring all the "waters" of transcendental reality. Let us look at what the Course says happens at this point.

We are told that "the Holy Spirit entered to abide with you" (T-19.IV(A).7:3), and that "His home is in your holy relationship" (T-19.IV(A).5:9); that "Heaven has entered quietly...and love has shined upon you, blessing your relationship with truth. God and His whole creation have entered it together" (T-18.I.11:2-3); that "love has entered your special relationship, and entered fully at your weak request" (T-18.VIII.12:1); that "Truth has rushed to meet you since you called upon it" (T-18.III.3:1); that "In your relationship the Holy Spirit has gently laid the real world; the world of happy dreams..." (T-18.II.9:4).

In addition to God, the Holy Spirit, Heaven, love, truth and the real world entering in, we are told that, as Helen and Bill experienced, Jesus is very personally present in the holy relationship: "You who hold your brother's hand also hold mine, for when you joined each other you were not alone" (T-18.III.4:1); "I hold your hand as surely as you agreed to take your brother's" (T-18.III.5:5); "This is a feast that honors your holy relationship....And I will join you there, as long ago I promised and promise still. For in your new relationship am I made welcome. And where I am made welcome, there I am" (T-19.IV(A).16:4-6).

What the inrush of all of this spirit does is instantly carry the relationship to a place of perfect, immaculate holiness, as this passage which we quoted earlier says:

> Your relationship with your brother has been uprooted

from the world of shadows, and its unholy purpose has been safely brought through the barriers of guilt, washed with forgiveness, and set shining and firmly rooted in the world of light (T-18.IX.13:1).

This, of course, does not happen on the conscious level. But on some deeper level of the minds of both people, the relationship becomes as holy as God Himself, totally free of resentment, judgment, avoidance, or the tiniest hint of separation. On this level you love each other "with a perfect love. Here is holy ground....Here you are joined in God, as much together as you are with Him" (T-18.I.9:3-5). In speaking of the ineffable beauty of this relationship, the Course almost breaks into song:

How lovely and how holy is your relationship, with the truth shining upon it! Heaven beholds it, and rejoices that you have let it come to you. The universe within you stands with you, together. And Heaven looks with love on what is joined in it, along with its Creator (T-18.I.11:4-8).

Beyond the bodies that you interposed between you, and shining in the golden light that reaches it from the bright, endless circle that extends forever, is your holy relationship, beloved of God Himself. How still it rests, in time and yet beyond, immortal yet on earth. How great the power that lies in it. Time waits upon its will, and earth will be as it would have it be....Every illusion brought to its forgiveness is gently overlooked and disappears. For at its center Christ has been reborn... (T-22.II.12:1-4,7-8).

In fact, as we saw in Chapter 1, this is why the Course classifies it as a holy relationship. It is holy because Holiness has entered it and purified it on an unconscious level. Whatever the two of you are demonstrating to each other, even if you are pulling each other's hair out, that holiness at the unconscious base of the relationship is what the relationship really is.

The setting of the goal

Of course, the Holy Spirit is well aware that your relationship is not at all like what we have just described above. And so this inner reality in which the two of you live in perfect oneness with each other, with all of the Sonship and with God, becomes the goal which the Holy Spirit sets for the relationship. The whole relationship now becomes about reaching the place that the relationship has actually already reached, unbeknownst to the partners' conscious minds.

Wait a minute, you say, I thought that we had set the goal for the relationship! What is this about the Holy Spirit setting it? These ideas are not in conflict, for you could say that your goal is an invitation and vehicle for the Holy Spirit's goal. If your goal is truly a common one, one that can be reached and shared together, then it is holy. Whatever its form, its content is holiness. It, then, becomes a vehicle for the goal of holiness, a container of something far greater than the two of you realize. This is exactly what happened with Helen and Bill. Their goal was simply a better way of interacting with people. What they received was something far beyond what they had imagined. They received *A Course in Miracles,* which did contain a better way of interacting, but also contained the goal of God Himself and a program for reaching that goal.

Yet your goal may also be an imperfect vehicle for His goal. There may be friction between yours and His. This is acknowledged in The Song of Prayer in its discussion of two people who join in prayer:

> Yet it is likely at first that what is asked for even by those who join in prayer is not the goal [of God, of holiness] that prayer should truly seek. Even together you may ask for [material] things, and thus set up but an illusion of a goal you share (S-1.IV.2:4-5).

Thus, your goal may have to go through refinements and purifications before it can be a perfect container of the goal of holiness. Until it does, your common purpose will not only not reflect the true goal, it will not be truly common, will not facilitate complete joining:

> Whatever resolutions patient and therapist reach in connection with their own divergent goals, they cannot become completely reconciled as one until they join with His [goal] (P-2.I.3:6).

Whatever the case is, your goal invited something larger into your relationship. When the two of you joined in common purpose, you—

perhaps unwittingly—signed a contract with God. And He is now the One at your ship's helm. He will steer it through all of its storms, keeping always in mind its ultimate goal as He sees it and in the end bringing it safely home to His chosen port.

What exactly is this goal? What does it mean to achieve holiness? Essentially, it means to come home to God together. "The goal you accepted is the goal of knowledge..." (T-18.III.2:3). "...you accepted truth as the goal for your relationship..." (T-17.VIII.6:1). In other words, your goal is Heaven. This is why the Course says, "You do not understand what you accepted," and then adds, "but remember that your understanding is not necessary" (T-18.III.4:11). This line from the Text says it best:

> God gave you and your brother Himself, and to remember this is now the only purpose that you share. And so it is the only one you have (T-24.I.7:5-6).

In the dream of time, it may be scores, hundreds or thousands of years before you achieve that goal. And you may not be physically together for that entire time. But even if you separate tomorrow, your destinies are now joined for good. And for the rest of the time you spend in the cosmic dream you will find your journeys overlapping and merging again and again, until you finally stand together in that place of perfect love and unity that was the Holy Spirit's goal for you.

The power of the goal

At this point your reaction may be that it is all well and good to have this wonderful goal. But what power is this goal going to exert in our relationship, especially considering that we may not even know about the existence of the goal of holiness? At this point it is very easy to see this goal as an impotent fantasy, floating somewhere up in the stratosphere; beautiful, but powerless in the face of the current destructive patterns that dominate the relationship. These patterns seem to be about as safe and secure as if they were locked in a bank vault. The goal is the thing that seems to be in danger; bound to soon be forgotten and left by the wayside. It seems virtually impossible that this goal will ever be fulfilled.

As usual, the Course reverses this view entirely. The goal is not a distant reality. On some level, as we saw, it is already realized. In fact, this realized goal is actually the reality of the relationship, a reality that will never change. Despite appearances, it is now what the relationship really and unchangeably is. And all of those unholy ego patterns that seem to dominate so much of the relationship, are now actually gone. The core of them, the belief in sin, has been removed: "Heaven has smiled upon [your relationship], and the belief in sin has been uprooted in its smile of love" (T-19.III.8:5). All that remains of it is a "feather of a wish," a "tiny illusion," a "microscopic remnant..." (T-19.IV(A).8:1).

> You see it still, because you do not realize that its foundation has gone. Its source has been removed, and so it can be cherished but a little while before it vanishes. Only the habit of looking for it still remains (T-19.III.8:6-8).

In other words, your egos are actually gone. Their roots have been pulled out. They just seem to be alive, like a fan that has been unplugged and hasn't quite stopped turning, or like a chicken whose head has been cut off, yet for a few seconds still runs around. It is only a matter of time before the fan stops, before the chicken falls over, before we realize that our egos are gone.

Also, from this point on, the goal will become an actual power in the relationship, something that will make its presence felt, something that will visibly take the relationship to places where it would never go otherwise. In fact, it is the goal that will draw the relationship to the place where it really is, to holiness. The following is one of the many places in which the Course speaks of the power of the goal:

> The goal's reality will call forth and accomplish every miracle needed for its fulfillment. Nothing too small or too enormous, too weak or too compelling, but will be gently turned to its use and purpose. The universe will serve it gladly, as it serves the universe. But do not interfere.
>
> The power set in you in whom the Holy Spirit's goal has been established is so far beyond your little conception of the infinite that you have no idea how great the strength that goes with you....its might...reaches past the stars and to the universe that lies beyond them... (T-17.VII.6:6-7:3).

In other words, it is a done deal. The power of the holy relationship is so great, and the weakness of all that would stand in its way so complete, that the fulfillment of the goal is utterly certain. The goal, as we have said, is already fulfilled. And the time in which both of you will realize that is on its way and certain to arrive. You might as well start celebrating now.

> There is a hush in Heaven, a happy expectancy, a little pause of gladness in acknowledgment of the journey's end....No illusions stand between you and your brother now. Look not upon the little wall of shadows [that seems to stand between you]. The sun has risen over it. How can a shadow keep you from the sun? (T-19.IV(A).6:1,3-5)

> How mighty can a little feather be before the great wings of truth? Can it oppose an eagle's flight, or hinder the advance of summer? Can it interfere with the effects of summer's sun upon a garden covered by snow? See but how easily this little wisp is lifted up and carried away, never to return....Would you not rather greet the summer sun than fix your gaze upon a disappearing snowflake, and shiver in remembrance of the winter's cold? (T-19.IV(A).9:1-4,6)

Examples of the power of the goal

On the practical level, what all this means is that once you and another person join in a common purpose, some spiritual Presence enters your relationship and becomes a very present guiding force. And this is not mere flowery rhetoric; this really happens.

Perhaps the perfect example was with Helen and Bill. When they joined in common purpose everything changed. That moment was the turning point of their lives. This was not so much a result of their own efforts in formulating and pursuing their goal; it was not because of the human side of that moment. It was exactly as the Course describes it: Their joining invited into their relationship a Presence. And it was this Presence that changed their lives forever, and the lives of many others. Within a short time after their instant of joining, this Presence began making Itself known, first through a series of inner visions which Helen had; and then Its influence flowered into the dictation of the Course. The really significant thing, then, was not the goal that they chose, but what that goal let into their relationship.

I have experienced much the same thing. Many years ago I had a very profound joining with someone who had been little more than a casual friend. For both of us it was overwhelming on a feeling level. Yet neither of us had any inkling of what had been set in motion on a spiritual level. It was almost like some kind of conception had taken place. And after a "gestation" of a few months, a spiritual community was born, one which has grown over the years and is still in progress. Little did we know it at the time, but in many ways the day on which we joined was the end of our lives as we had known them and the beginning of something new, a journey we had never planned to take. From that time on it seemed that some Presence had been let in the back door of our lives, a Presence which made Itself tangibly known. It began by rearranging our two lives and then started drawing the lives of others into this thing. And It has remained. After all the time that has passed, and all the changes we have gone through—including raising our separate families—we are both very conscious that at the center of our relationship is Something that just does not go away, Something with a mind of Its own and a definite plan of its own. We don't really know exactly where It is leading us. But we seem to be along for the ride, for apparently It is here to stay.

The Christ child

The Course sees the most enormous significance in the holy relationship. Once it is formed, it is out of its center that our salvation will come. From now on, the relationship will be our light, for in it the light has been reborn. The Course refers many times to the fact that our salvation will come out of the holy relationship, at one point calling it quite plainly "the source of your salvation" (T-20.VIII.6:9). In a striking passage we are told that, "In this world, God's Son comes closest to himself in a holy relationship" (20.V.1:1). In other words, we most fully discover our true nature when joined with another, for our true nature is not individual. "A holy relationship is one in which you join with what is part of you in truth" (T-21.IV.3:5). The person that you join with is as much a part of your true Identity as you are.

Yet again, this is all so hard to believe. The mundane, perhaps unpromising, appearance of the relationship seems so much more real than what the Course is saying is its reality. You may often find yourself thinking: How can this relationship really offer me everything? How can it be that I will actually find God through my union with this person (especially given what a jerk this person is)?

The Course's answer to this dichotomy between appearance and reality is to use the metaphor of the Christ child. By allowing Holiness to enter the relationship, yet not allowing it to fully enter on the conscious level, it seems that Holiness has come to you faintly, as something small, weak and fragile. Yet this is really the illusion. This faint light, this barely detectable spiritual force that has entered your relationship is really not small and weak at all. It is the Christ Himself. He is the One Who has come to you. Your joining has allowed Him to be reborn at the center of your relationship. He is your relationship. And even though He seems to be but a fragile infant, He is the bringer of your salvation and carries with Him all the power and might of God. He does not need you to take care of Him; He will take care of you.

> The infancy of salvation is carefully guarded by love, preserved from every thought that would attack it, and quietly made ready to fulfill the mighty task for which it was given you. Your newborn purpose is nursed by angels, cherished by the Holy Spirit and protected by God Himself. It needs not your protection; it is yours. For it is deathless, and within it lies the end of death....What has been given you, even in its infancy, is in full communication with God and you. In its tiny hands it holds, in perfect safety, every miracle you will perform, held out to you. The miracle of life is ageless, born in time but nourished in eternity. Behold this infant, to whom you gave a resting place by your forgiveness of your brother, and see in it the Will of God. Here is the babe of Bethlehem reborn. And everyone who gives him shelter will follow him, not to the cross, but to the resurrection and the life (T-19.IV(C).9:3-6,10:4-9).

~4~
The Period of Discomfort

A s wonderful as the moment of joining can be, like all moments of release from the ego, it is initially short-lived. What has happened is that we have temporarily left our egos behind and experienced a tiny bit of what lies beyond them. Even though what we experienced was so wonderful, and even though our joining unleashed a "light far brighter than the sun that lights the sky you see" (T-22.VI.4:1), our egos are still sitting there waiting for us to return. And they only allow so much vacation time. When we momentarily disconnected from our egos, the understanding they had was that they were allowing us a brief interlude, a one-night stand, a little fling to satiate our annoying hunger for God.

Yet that was a fatal error, for God is not comfortable with just having His foot in the door. The blazing light that was unleashed in our relationship, once it has entered, wants *all* of the relationship, and all of *us*. It wants to completely replace the egoic basis for the relationship, leaving no trace of it. As we saw in the last chapter, it has already done that on a deeper level, and it wants to extend that to the conscious level.

And so now the relationship most probably enters a very difficult time, which the Course calls the "period of discomfort" (T-20.VII.2:1). For the ego and the Holy Spirit are both powerful influences in it, and both want all of it. There is a wonderful section about this period, called "The Healed Relationship," in Chapter 17. What we are told in this section is that there now begins an incredible tension between the holiness that the relationship has accepted into its center—which is here called the "goal"—and the conscious condition of the relationship—which is here called the "structure" of the relationship. As we saw, joining in common purpose has allowed the goal of holiness to enter in and become an actual operative force in the relationship. On some level, you—and your ego—sense its presence. Yet the conscious structure of the relationship is still strongly ego-based. Thus, the goal and the structure of the relationship are completely at odds with each other, producing an enormous conflict. "The Healed

Relationship" discusses the effects of this conflict as well as how to resolve it.

I can personally vouch for the experience of this period of discomfort, having been through it in many relationships. In my experience, when you join, you feel that for once something real has happened to you, something set apart from the blurry dream that you have spent your life wandering through. You sense that the relationship has been touched by a higher hand and granted a higher purpose, that this relationship will be a large part of fulfilling your whole reason for being here.

And so you get tremendously invested in the relationship—and so does your ego. For if this is what your life is going to be about, if this is what is going to fulfill your dreams, then you either do it the ego's way or the ego is out. The ego's need to control the relationship is intensified by the fact that you sense something at the center of the relationship that is so alien to the ego that there is literally no room for it. Thus, the ego's head is really on the chopping block here. If it does not gain control of the relationship, it will have to watch as you go on to adopt a whole new way of being, leaving behind all that you think you are—leaving behind the ego itself.

So the ego lunges in and the relationship suddenly becomes choked with the ego's hopes and dreams, as well as its demands. You start demonstrating all kinds of crazy patterns that are often more egoic than what you display in your normal, *unholy* relationships. And this makes the relationship seem absolutely absurd. It starts looking like a bad joke. Here you both know you are together for a higher purpose. You know that at the core of your relationship you have touched the Real, that there is authentic and beautiful love there, a love that transcends what normally passes for love in this world. And yet for the life of you you cannot seem to reach that place. It begins to seem absolutely impossible that you could actually live from the place you experienced in that moment of joining. The whole situation seems ridiculous. As the Course says, "As these two contemplate their relationship from the point of view of this new purpose, they are inevitably appalled" (T-17.V.5:6).

There are many reactions that naturally follow at this point. To begin with, you lose faith that you will ever reach the goal. To some extent, I think this is almost inevitable. Also, you start to blame your partner for this distressing turn of events: "You will find many opportunities to blame your brother for the 'failure' of your relationship..." (T-17.V.8:2). And you begin to find ways—several ways—to avoid the person and withdraw from the relationship. Let's face it, you tell yourself, this situation is hopeless.

Why even try? All of these are very important themes that the Course deals with at length and which we will be covering in this chapter.

Yet there is a critically important purpose for this period. And, ironically, it has to do with the very thing that causes the discomfort: the stark contrast between the goal of the relationship and its current structure. This contrast may be painful, yet it has the wonderful effect of placing you in "a crisis of decision" (a phrase that Rudolf Bultmann used to describe the effect of the historical Jesus). It puts you in a situation in which the only real way out is to commit to the goal of holiness.

How does it do this? First, of course, it makes it very clear what the alternatives are and that you must choose only one. "The conflict between the goal and the structure of the relationship is so apparent that they cannot coexist" (T-17.V.4:3). Then, it makes the goal the only viable alternative, for somewhere inside you know that the goal is not going to go away, whereas the current structure *can*. Thus, if you commit to the current structure of the relationship you will stay in conflict. Only committing to the goal will free you. As the Course says:

> Yet now the goal will not be changed. Set firmly in the unholy relationship, there is no course except to change the relationship to fit the goal. Until this happy solution is seen and accepted as the only way out of the conflict, the relationship may seem to be severely strained (T-17.V.4:4-6).

The point is that once God has gotten His foot in the door, there is no going back. Once you have seen the light, trying to turn away from it just makes the pain worse. Thus, as much as you may hate this fact and resist it, as attached as you may be to your ego, the only real choice you have at this point is to commit yourself to leaving the ego behind.

And so this stark contrast between the goal and the structure gives us a golden opportunity to take a real stand against our egos and for the Holy Spirit. We may never face this choice as clearly and unavoidably as we do when we enter the period of discomfort in the holy relationship. Here we can really feel the promise that the Holy Spirit holds out to us, and can really see the insanity of attacking someone in whom we saw such transcendent beauty. This is why this period is really a kindness and not an unjust burden, and why the following challenging passage is absolutely right:

> It would not be kinder to shift the goal more slowly,

for the contrast would be obscured, and the ego given time to reinterpret each slow step according to its liking. Only a radical shift in purpose could induce a complete change of mind about what the whole relationship is for (T-17,V.5:1-2).

Yet still, even if we commit to the goal, how do we actually get there? It still seems like an impossibility.

The goal will provide the means

A goal is reached by means. The means for the goal of getting back to God together is what the Course calls Christ's vision. Through Christ's vision we see the reality of the goal in each other, the face of Christ in each other; we see our partner as sinless. In other words, we forgive each other. This is not the forgiveness of a particular thing that the other said or did. It is the overlooking of his or her entire appearance as a separate mind living in a body. It means seeing past the illusion of the *homo sapien* and consistently gazing on a light that is not of this world. It is therefore something that generally comes over a long period of time. It is a process, and one that has many aspects to it. And so all of what we cover in the rest of this chapter will be different aspects of the forgiveness process as the Course sees it.

Unfortunately, the means—seeing our partner as sinless—can seem very nearly as impossible as the goal itself. Yet the Course makes us a wonderful promise. It tells us that just as the goal was given to us, so the means will be given us as well. In fact, it is the goal that will give us the means. And to make this possible, all it asks of us is the same small willingness that enabled us to join in the first place.

All we need to do, says the Course, is just *be willing* to see our partner as sinless. That's it. If we just fulfill that single requirement, then Christ's vision will be granted us. We will be given vision to see the holy in the other person. And since this is the means to our goal, the goal will be reached and complete salvation will be ours.

And so, from the Course's standpoint, we cannot claim that the means are actually difficult. How can they be when they are given to us? If we are experiencing them as difficult, it cannot be because *they* are difficult, but because *we* are resisting them. In other words, we do not want them. And the only reason that we could not want the means is that we do not want the goal to which they lead. Yet, the Course reminds us, we *do* want the goal, for we invited it. So the problem is not with the means, it is our own inner division, our own inconsistency:

> You recognize you want the goal. Are you not also willing to accept the means? If you are not, let us admit that you are inconsistent. A purpose is attained by means, and if you want a purpose you must be willing to want the means as well (T-20.VII.2:3-6).

So how do we come to want the means? How do we practice the willingness to see our partner sinless? The following are some suggestions from the Course's discussions of the holy relationship.

Remember the inestimable value of your partner

The Course has the most amazing things to say about the value of our partner. It says that he is literally our savior, for we will only come to believe in our innocence by seeing it reflected in his eyes. Think about this: If you have joined with someone in common purpose, that person now possesses a role in your journey to God analogous to the role ascribed to Jesus in the Christian tradition. Imagine the gratitude you would feel if you really believed this. This is the person who is going to free you from the ego by seeing more than an ego in you. You are not going to believe in the light in you by just seeing it yourself. Someone else will have to see it, too. And you are not going to believe what he sees until you see the same light in him.

> He has in him the power to forgive your sin, as you for him. Neither can give it to himself alone. And yet your savior stands beside each one....Would you not offer him forgiveness, when only he can offer it to you? For his redemption he will give you yours, as surely as God created every living thing and loves it (T-19.IV(D).13:5-7,15:2-3).

What this means is that everything hinges on the one choice of how we choose to see our partner. The whole crux of the relationship lies in this choice, and the whole of our salvation lies in this relationship. So our entire awakening to God literally hinges on this single choice: Do we want to see our partner as sinful or sinless? For this reason the Course urges us over and over to not make this choice lightly: "Think carefully how you would look upon the giver of this gift..." (T-19.IV(D).20:1); "Think carefully before you let yourself use faithlessness against him" (T-17.VIII.5:3).

To make this choice aright, we must be willing to face the enormous discrepancy between how we currently see this person and her true role as our savior, between the judgment we so easily accord to her now and the overwhelming gratitude that we really owe her. And we must be willing to admit that we are in no position to judge her value, for, in fact, our ego has completely blinded us to who she really is:

> It is impossible to overestimate your brother's value....What is inestimable clearly cannot be evaluated. Do you recognize the fear that rises from the meaningless attempt to judge what lies so far beyond your judgment you cannot even see it? Judge not what is invisible to you or you will never see it, but wait in patience for its coming (T-20.V.3:1,3-5).

Faith in your brother

As soon as you join with another in a common goal your condemnation of him takes a very concrete and identifiable form: *You lack faith in him to do his part in reaching the goal.* This is one of the most visible symptoms of the ego in a holy relationship. Yet it seems very rational: "Of course I believe in the Christ within that person. But that still does not mean that he is going to make the right choices. How can I know that he is going to hold up his end and reach the goal with me?" The Course, however, has something very different to say about this:

> If you lack faith in anyone to fulfill, and perfectly, his part in any situation dedicated in advance to truth, your dedication is divided (T-17.VII.6:2).

That is a pretty strong statement. If you do not trust your partner to get there with you, your dedication is divided. You are dedicated to the truth in him, or you would not be in this common venture with him, and you are dedicated to illusions in him, or you would trust him to get there with you.

Why is faith in our partner warranted? Why can we trust that he will fulfill his part perfectly? I think the answer to this is really very simple. Faith in our partner is warranted because of who he really is. Faithlessness comes from seeing him as a faulty, limited mind stuck in a frail, mortal body. Who could have faith in a being like that? But that is not who our partner is. To get in touch with who he really is, I have found the following exercise useful.

Imagine that 2,000 years ago someone somehow succeeded in drugging Jesus (this does not make sense to me, but for the sake of the exercise, try to suspend your disbelief for a moment). Someone gave him megadoses of all kinds of mind-dulling and mind-warping drugs. As a result, he fell into a profound stupor, forgot who he was, and started acting just as neurotic as the rest of us. These hypothetical drugs were so powerful that they have still not worn off. He is still wandering the earth in such a stupor that he is acting like a normal, anxiety-ridden human. And, lo and behold, he has wandered into your life as your holy relationship partner. For a moment try to actually imagine this about your partner, that he or she is really Jesus drugged—still a being of unspeakable holiness and majesty, still the infinitely beautiful Son of God, still the savior of the world, merely in a drug-induced stupor.

Now ask yourself: Do you trust this being to make it home with you in the end? Do you have faith that his or her choices will, in the long run, lead him in the right direction? Is this person someone you can count on? I think most of us would answer "yes"—if we could really imagine this person being Jesus drugged. This, I believe, is the answer to why we can have faith in our partner. If we do not have faith, we do not know who our partner really is.

Now, having faith that our partner will reach the goal with us does not mean that we trust him to make the right choice in every situation. It just means that we trust him to make it to the end with us. Along the way there is room for plenty of mistakes, and each of us will make a bundle. This is a given; it is no big deal. Our partner is ultimately trustable even in the face of his mistakes. A drugged Jesus will make a lot of foolish choices but his natural affinity for home will overcome them all in the end.

I think that another one of the thoughts you can practice to strengthen your faith is to remember the beautiful person you experienced when you joined, and realize that *that* person can be trusted to go the distance with you. Even if you have lost sight of that person, and even if she herself has, she is still in there, still dedicated to the same goal and still supported by the same strength of God in seeking it.

One thing that may help this is to change our focus. It is a natural ego tendency to focus on all the ways in which our partner is falling short. Instead, we can consciously choose to focus on the ways in which she is really demonstrating her fidelity to our common goal, really doing her part to reach it with us. The following is a wonderful passage about this:

> Although you may have made many mistakes since [you invited the Holy Spirit into your relationship], you have also made enormous efforts to help Him do His work. And He has not been lacking in appreciation for all you have done for Him. Nor does He see the mistakes at all. Have you been similarly grateful to your brother? Have you consistently appreciated the good efforts, and overlooked mistakes? Or has your appreciation flickered and grown dim in what seemed to be the light of the mistakes? Perhaps you are now entering upon a campaign to blame him for the discomfort of the situation in which you find yourself (T-17.V.11:3-9).

It may seem obvious to us that *we* can be depended on to go the distance, whereas our partner is clearly a gamble. Yet one very interesting thing that the Course says about our lack of faith in our partner is that it really is a lack of faith in ourselves:

> Yet think on this, and learn the cause of faithlessness: You think you hold against your brother what he has done to you. But what you really blame him for is what you did to him. It is not his past but yours you hold against him. And you lack faith in him because of what you were (T-17.VII.8:1-4).

This is a deep psychological truth. One way to look at this is that somewhere inside we realize that the relationship deserves only our undivided love and faith. Yet we see ourselves constantly falling short. We do not have faith in ourselves to achieve the goal. And this produces a terrible sense of guilt in us. How do we get rid of this guilt? We fool ourselves into dumping onto our partner the responsibility for our own ego reactions and for the relationship itself: "It is her fault that I am angry at her. It is her fault that the relationship is going so poorly." We have simply projected onto her our own lack of faith in ourselves. We are afraid that if we admit the responsibility we truly have for our own feelings and for the relationship, then we will have to face how hopeless and guilty we are. Yet we are just as mistaken about ourselves as we are about our partner. We, too, can be trusted to make it through to the end.

Alas, faithlessness is one of those unavoidables in the infant holy relationship. Yet, thankfully, it is not on our shoulders to acquire faith. Faith in our brother is part of Christ's vision. As such, it is one of those things that will be given us by the Holy Spirit. All that He asks is that we consistently choose to lay our faithlessness aside. I think the Course has a wonderful attitude toward this. In speaking of faithlessness, it says:

> You will make this error, but be not at all concerned with that. The error does not matter. Faithlessness brought to faith will never interfere with truth....Use not your faithlessness. Let it enter and look upon it calmly, but do not use it....Accept not the illusion of peace it offers, but look upon its offering and recognize it is illusion (T-17.VIII.3:7-9,5:3-4,9).

In other words, of course you will feel a lack of faith in your brother. It is a given; no big deal. As the above passage says, it "does not matter." Just let those feelings enter, but do not fuel them. Do not add your mental assent to them and do not act upon them. Just look on them calmly, see them as meaningless and unwanted, see them as illusion, and give them over to the Holy Spirit. And, in exchange, He will give you faith.

Substitution, avoidance and withdrawal

As we have said, the only way out of the conflict between the goal and the structure of the relationship is to choose the goal. Yet we lack faith that the relationship can actually make it to the goal. And so, the only solution *seems* to be obvious. We in some way must try to squirm out of the relationship.

Of course, the most extreme form this takes is that we actually cut off the relationship, either in whole or in large measure:

> Now the ego counsels thus; substitute for this another relationship to which your former goal was quite

appropriate. You can escape from your distress only by getting rid of your brother. You need not part entirely if you choose not to do so. But you must exclude major areas of fantasy from each other, to save your sanity (T-17.V.7:1-4).

The Course responds to this with some of the most emphatic language it ever uses. For in this seemingly reasonable act of disconnecting from a "hopeless" relationship, we are casually throwing away salvation itself. Here is the Course's response:

> *Hear not this now!* Have faith in Him Who answered you. He heard....Now He asks for faith a little longer, even in bewilderment. For this will go, and you will see the justification for your faith emerge, to bring you shining conviction. Abandon Him not now, nor one another. This relationship has been reborn as holy (T-17.V.7:5-7,11-14).

In other words, just gut it out. As long as your joint purpose remains intact, trust the relationship, no matter how hard it gets, no matter where it is at. Trust its changes, its rhythms, its mountains and its valleys. Trust it whatever form it takes and wherever it leads you. Remember, here is the baby Jesus reborn. He is the hope of the world. And you are his parents. Do not abandon him, even if he takes you to the ends of the earth— or the ends of your patience.

Yet there is an important qualifier in this: "as long as your joint purpose remains intact." This is a highly subjective matter, but in my experience, it is not particularly fuzzy. When that purpose is still intact, regardless of all the storms in the relationship, there is something solid at its center. And this solidness can be felt. Yet in some holy relationships there comes a certain point in which one or both people have given up on the relationship. I do not think it is a decision that is made in the conscious mind or in a moment. It is a very deep-level decision that is pointless to try to challenge. When this happens, you can feel that this deep solidness that united you is now completely out of range. Where there was this unspoken, unquestioned bond between you, there is now just empty space. It feels like you are in different worlds, speaking different languages. At this point, for all intents and purposes, you have separated. And it will only be a matter of time before you physically separate. It really is best to let the relationship go in peace. Yet at the same time, great discernment needs to be exercised in making this decision, for the Course clearly indicates that separating for ego reasons, separating *because* the joint purpose remains intact (and threatens your egos), will be a great temptation.

According to the Course, many will yield to this temptation: "Many relationships have been broken off at this point, and the pursuit of the old goal re-established in another relationship" (T-17.V.3:8). Does this negate all that the Course has said about how the person and the Spirit can be implicitly trusted to bring the relationship to its goal? No, I do not think so. What this means is that there has simply been a delay. As the Course says,

> ...nor is what appears to be the end of the relationship a real end. Again, each has learned the most he can at the time. Yet all who meet will someday meet again, for it is the destiny of all relationships to become holy. God is not mistaken in His Son (M-3.4:4-7).

So, everyone who unites in common purpose, yet seems to lose sight of their goal and separate, will someday reunite and reach the place they glimpsed from afar in that original moment. It may not be in this life, it may not be in this millennium. But the Spirit never forgets. When a common goal is reached, a pact is made for all eternity.

I remember several years ago I experienced the apparent break-up of what I believed to be a holy relationship. I was in a state of depression over what I thought was the failure of a relationship of immeasurable promise. One night I was in a Course study group, and for some strange reason we all decided to sit on the floor that night, the only time we ever did that. During the meeting one of the members—who knew nothing of my situation—began talking about how even if a relationship breaks up it will someday get back together again and succeed. I then remembered the above passage from the Manual, and for the first time made the connection that this relationship did not really fail; someday we would do all that we had been promised that we would. It was a great feeling. The significance of this washed over me like a wave. And just at that moment a fairly large earthquake hit the area. Since we were sitting on the floor we all felt it very directly. Whatever the fact was, it sure felt like a thunderous confirmation of what I had just realized.

Yet, even if we do not actually leave the relationship, there are several other ways in which we can subtly, or not so subtly, disconnect. We may withdraw emotionally. We may decide to hide our thoughts from our partner. When we experience problems in the relationship, we may try to split them off from the relationship and solve them somewhere else: "Confronted with any aspect of the situation that seems to be difficult, the ego will attempt to take this aspect elsewhere, and resolve it there" (T-17.VI.7:1). I think this probably refers to is two phenomena. One is where we have a problem with our partner, and "solve" it by going off and complaining about it to someone else, hoping to come away with the feeling that we have been vindicated. This obviously does not solve anything (though it sure can yield a momentary pleasure).

The other is where we have a particular problem area in our relationship, and we try to solve it by finding another relationship in which to meet our unfulfilled need. Of course our relationships are going to take different forms. With our holy relationship partner it may not be appropriate to read the Course together, for instance, while that may be perfectly appropriate with someone else. I do not think this is what the Course is talking about. What it is speaking to here, I believe, is where something lies unhealed in a relationship, and rather than seek its healing, we merely go somewhere else to try to fill that hole in us. We try to find satisfaction somewhere else to offset the pain we are finding in the one relationship. This clearly implies that healing is not possible in that relationship. It says we have no faith that real solution can be found, so let us go find it with someone else.

The Course has essentially the same thing to say about all of these methods of withdrawal, whether they be leaving the relationship and transferring attention to another relationship, withdrawing emotionally or mentally, or taking aspects of the relationship into other situations to solve them there. All of these are what it calls substitution:

> To substitute is to accept instead...to choose between, renouncing one aspect of the Sonship in favor of the other....substitution is the strongest defense the ego has for separation (T-18.I.1:1,3,6).

In other words, the ego is saying to you, "Get rid of this situation (or this part of it), because it is just too hard, too hopeless; and go over here where the grass is greener." This, of course, is simply an expression of your lack of faith in your partner and in the power of the goal. It is your faithlessness whispering in your ear.

The Course has some very interesting things to say about this. We are told that instead of carrying problems in the relationship off to be solved somewhere else, we need to take them all and carry them to the center of the relationship, where Christ has been reborn. There, in the holy light of our union, are all problems already shined away. "For in the miracle of your holy relationship...is every miracle contained" (T-19.IV(A).5:2).

Therefore, says the Course, the problem was not what you thought it was. The only problem was your lack of faith, for "There is no problem in any situation that faith will not solve" (T-17.VII.2:1). It is your faithlessness that prompted you to separate off the supposed problem from the answer, thus blinding you to the fact that the problem had already been solved. As the Course says, "Is it not possible that all your problems have been solved, but you have removed yourself from the solution?" (T-17.VII.2:4)

Instead of using other situations to steal away portions of the holy relationship, leaving it isolated and fragmented, the Course counsels the exact reverse. It says that we should make *every* situation a vessel for the *entirety* of our holy relationship, something which the Holy Spirit has already done:

> There is no situation that does not involve your whole relationship, in every aspect and complete in every part....When the Holy Spirit changed the purpose of your relationship by exchanging yours for His, the goal He placed there was extended to every situation in which you enter, or will ever enter (T-17.VII.8:11,9:5).

How we follow the Holy Spirit's lead here and actually apply this truth ourselves will be discussed in the next section.

Total and unswerving focus on the goal

In the Course's discussions of the holy relationship, a very interesting attitude emerges about how to pursue the goal. It is an attitude that sounds remarkably like what you would hear from some motivational speaker who is teaching you how to sell a whole lot of real estate. Yet, this is an attitude that re-emerges very strongly in the Workbook. I do not know why this should surprise me. If these basic attitudes can work in pursuing the goal of money, power or physical health, why should they not be of use in pursuing God? True, the Course balances these methods out with a healthy dose of trust in the Holy Spirit and relinquishment of ego, but given that balancing, the Course is definitely not against using a little willpower.

To set the stage, we are told that, "Every situation in which you find yourself is but a means to meet the purpose set for your relationship" (T-17.VII.5:1). In other words, we should see every situation—whether our partner is physically there or not—as a kind of exercise room in which we can attain the goal of our relationship. We are reminded that we should make the choice to see it that way "in each situation separately, until you can more safely look beyond each situation, in an understanding far broader than you now possess" (T-17.VI.1:7).

This has some very specific implications for how we enter each situation, and this is where the Course starts sounding like a motivational speaker:

> In any situation in which you are uncertain, the first thing to consider, very simply, is "What do I want to come of this? What is it for?" The clarification of the goal belongs at the beginning, for it is this which will determine the outcome....Without a clear-cut, positive goal, set at the outset, the situation just seems to happen, and makes no sense....No goal was set with which to bring the means in line....The value of deciding in advance what you want to happen is simply that you will perceive the situation as a means to make it happen. You will therefore make every effort to overlook what interferes with the accomplishment of your objective, and concentrate on everything that helps you meet it (T-17.VI.2:1-3,3:1,5,4:1-2).

What I get from this is that I should say to myself at the beginning of a situation: "This situation is simply a means for meeting the goal of my holy relationship. I will use the situation to cultivate the willingness to see my partner as sinless. This is the only reason I am here and the only aim of my effort." Now, of course, this need not take the form of concentrating only on your holy relationship partner and ignoring everyone who has not consciously joined with you in common purpose—far from it. Obviously, seeing anyone as sinless—or making any choice for God, for that matter— directly benefits seeing your holy relationship partner as sinless, which in turn helps you to see everyone as sinless.

Now normally we enter situations without a clear-cut goal. We wait for the situation to tell us what it is about. This, says the Course, is the ego's procedure. And what it results in is the situation ruling over us. Whatever the outer outcome is, it will simply drag our emotions along in its wake, "for the ego believes the situation brings the experience" (T-17.VI.5:8). Yet if we enter the situation with a clear goal in mind, and use the situation only on behalf of that goal, then our experience of the situation will be an experience of the goal—regardless of the outer events. "If the situation is used for truth and sanity, its outcome must be peace. And this is quite apart from what the outcome *is*" (T-17.VI.5:2-3).

Overall, the Course suggests that we maintain an unswerving focus on the goal, concentrating on everything that facilitates it and overlooking everything that interferes with it. Putting this together with the method for dealing with our faithlessness which we discussed earlier, we get a very helpful overall philosophy for moving toward our goal. We simply stay riveted on the goal of holiness. Do not relax the goal, do not water it down. Maintain its stark contrast with everything that is not it. Do not make excuses. And when interferences naturally arise—resentments, judgments, irritations, anger, withdrawal—look on them calmly, realize they are no big deal, acknowledge that their only significance is that they interfere with the goal, and let them go into the Holy Spirit's hands.

I almost picture a man walking through underbrush, intent only on reaching an all-important destination. As each branch or frond looms in front of him, its only significance is that it is in his way. It is not a bad thing; it is expected. In fact, the branch is not important enough to be bad, or even to really be examined. It is only important enough to require the acknowledgment that it is there and the effort to brush it aside.

Although we will occasionally encounter larger obstacles that require more attention, this can be our basic *modus operandi* in the holy relationship, and in life.

The holy instant and ACIM conflict resolution

A holy instant could be defined as a moment of disconnecting from the past and entering fully into the present, of disconnecting from the ego's way of seeing and being momentarily open to a new way. According to the Course, the holy relationship was formed in just such a moment, when two people disconnected from their habitual belief in separate interests. It was in that instant that the relationship was made anew. In that instant the power was released that will ultimately bring the relationship to its goal.

Yet when you attack each other, you obscure that instant of union and cut yourself off from the power that it unleashed. The original moment of your joining has stayed with you and still lights your way, but your attacks make it seem distant, powerless and irrelevant:

> The experience of an instant, however compelling it may be, is easily forgotten if you allow time to close over it. It must be kept shining and gracious in your awareness of time, but not concealed within it. The instant remains. But where are you? To give thanks to one another is to appreciate the holy instant, and thus enable its results to be accepted and shared. To attack your brother is not to lose the instant, but to make it powerless in its effects (T-17.V.12).

So what do you do when you get into some kind of argument, unpleasant exchange or knock-down-drag-out fight? The universal tendency is to want to stay in the battleground and solve the problem from there. Perhaps you hope to solve it through winning the war, or maybe you will wave your white flag and surrender, or perhaps you will both sit down at the peace table and each agree to a series of conditions that will keep the other at bay.

Instead, the Holy Spirit asks that you accept a holy instant.

> When you feel the holiness of your relationship is threatened by anything, stop instantly and offer the Holy Spirit your willingness, in spite of fear, to let Him exchange this instant for the holy one that you would rather have (T-18.V.VI.1).

In other words, disconnect from the battleground (you may want to read a beautiful description of this in T-23.IV.5-6). Rise above it. Stand outside of its rules and objectives. Leave behind its history, the chain of events which "caused" it. In short, stop what you are doing. Stop talking. Stop trying to solve it in your way, which means on *its* terms. Pull your mind fully into the motionless present. Calmly affirm that your current emotions are literally insane. Invite the Holy Spirit into your mind, and ask to see the situation with Him. The Course gives us a beautiful prayer with which to do this, one that I have found exceedingly helpful:

I desire this holy instant for myself,
that I may share it with my brother, whom I love.
It is not possible that I can have it without him,
or he without me.
Yet it is wholly possible for us to share it now.
And so I choose this instant as the one to offer to the Holy
Spirit,
that His blessing may descend on us,
and keep us both in peace (T-18.V.7:3-6).

The Course is giving us here a concrete exercise in conflict resolution. I therefore suggest that we really do it. When we feel the holiness of our relationship threatened by anything, we can stop (we may need to excuse ourselves from the room) and use this prayer, saying each word with full awareness of its meaning, saying it again until we feel our anger lift and peace come over us. I see this as a radical and brilliant method of conflict resolution and would therefore like to draw out some of its aspects:

The conflict is not healed by solving it on its level

- Whoever is saner stops instantly.
- You stop trying to solve the conflict in the usual way, on its level.

Conflict is healed by letting go of the belief-system underlying the conflict

- You forget about the conflict, its nature, its history, who did what, who thinks and feels what, etc.
- You realize the conflict is not between yourself and the other person,
- ...that there is no threat or problem outside of you that requires your response in order to make yourself safe
- ...that the problem is in your own mind; that it is your own perception of conflict and outer threat that needs healing.

...and by entering the holy instant

- Your perception of conflict and solution always places happiness in the future, at the end of a process.
- Yet you can have happiness *now* by entering the holy instant.

A unilateral process

- This process is undertaken by one person, "whoever is saner at the time."
- There is thus no demand for the other person to cooperate in the same process, and in fact no need for it.

One does it for both, as a gift to both

- You do this, however, not only for yourself but for the other, recognizing that if one is in fear, both will be in fear; but if one accepts a holy instant, both will be healed.
- So you accept a holy instant for yourself, not out of anger and withdrawal from the other, but out of love and gratitude for the other. You do it knowing that you can express your love and gratitude by bringing healing to both right now.
- Thus, being saner is not seen as making one a righteous victim of the other's insanity. It is seen as a gift one can bestow on the other, the other who is loved so much.

~ ~ ~

By entering the holy instant, rather than trying to "work out" the conflict as we perceive it, we can catch a glimpse of our true relationship, which is already "raised above the battleground, in it no more" (T-23.IV.4:5); the holy relationship that is obscured by our day-to-day functioning. There, we come once again and "stand at the same altar where grace was laid for both of you....There will you see the miracle of your relationship as it was made again through faith" (T-19.I.13:4,14:3).

Here, then, is everything. Here is the loveliness of your relationship, with means and end in perfect harmony already. Here is the perfect faith that you will one day offer to your brother already offered you; and here the limitless forgiveness you will give each other already given, the face of Christ you yet will look upon already seen (T-20.V.6:5-7).

In the holy instant, then, we can catch a brief glimpse of the goal of the relationship, already accomplished. "The change of purpose the Holy Spirit brought to your relationship has in it all the effects that you will see. They can be looked at *now*. Why wait till they unfold in time and fear they may not come, although already there?" (T-26.VIII.6:3-5)

Thus, the relationship needs to be frequently renewed in holy instants, especially when things get painful. For the holy instant is its home. By practicing what we discussed earlier—making holiness the goal of each situation—the Course says that we can "make a holy instant of every situation" (T-17.VIII.3:1).

And then the power of the Holy Spirit's purpose is free to use instead. This power instantly transforms all situations into one sure and continuous means for establishing His purpose, and demonstrating its reality (T-17.VIII.3:3-4).

Overlooking the body

In most relationships, the body looms very large in how we see our partner. This will be true also of the infant holy relationship, especially if it includes romance. Yet releasing this focus on the body is one of the primary tasks we have in achieving the goal of the relationship. The Course has some very strong things to say about the body, things which sure seem like sacrifice to those of us who are invested in the body. Yet (I keep telling myself) they are only sacrifice if our identity is nothing more than a body.

What the Course says about the body is in the end extremely logical. First, we are told, in essence, that to the extent that the relationship is based on the body, it is not a relationship. For you cannot have a relationship with a body; the body is not a person. It is a thing, an object. It is like having a relationship with one of those life-size inflatable dolls.

Not only is the body an object, it is an enclosure. Like a safe, it was made to hide things, to protect things. Specifically, it was made to keep the mind—its thoughts, its emotions, its attitudes and its aspirations—*private*, secret. And privacy and joining are antithetical. The body was made to separate you from others.

So the body is an object with which you cannot have a relationship, and which is designed to hide the mind and thus thwart real relationship. Having a relationship with it is like going to visit someone with a ten-foot wall around his house, and then never going inside the gate, but instead stopping at the wall and trying to have a visit with *it*. The Course puts it a little more strongly:

> Any relationship in which the body enters is based not on love, but on idolatry. Love wishes to be known, completely understood and shared. It has no secrets; nothing that it would keep apart and hide....
> The Holy Spirit's temple is not a body, but a relationship. The body is an isolated speck of darkness; a hidden secret room, a tiny spot of senseless mystery, a meaningless enclosure carefully protected, yet hiding nothing....The Holy Spirit does not build His temples where love can never be (T-20.VI.2:4-6,5:1-2,6).

Now the Course is *not* saying that we should not use our bodies in a relationship. For that would not only rule out sex, that would even get rid of talking! No, because we largely gather information by using our physical senses, the body is for now an important instrument in a relationship. It becomes the way in which we can demonstrate to our partner's senses all the love we feel for her inside. It becomes the instrument that we use to allow our minds to bridge the apparent distance between them. As the Course says, "In the service of uniting [the body] becomes a beautiful lesson in communion..." (T-8.VII.3:4). And so the Course is not at all ruling out any bodily activity. It is just urging us to reinterpret the purpose we give those activities. In them, it is asking, is the body seen as an end in itself or simply as a communication device?

Yet—and here is the challenging part—used purely as a tool for communication between minds, the body becomes neutral, inconsequential, purely functional. It becomes, in essence, no different from a telephone. And when you are about to call someone you love, you do not think, "Boy, I can't wait to get my hands on that gorgeous telephone, with its shiny white plastic and those cute little tones it makes when you push its buttons." You are just glad that it works and can serve its function of allowing you to communicate. If what you truly want is to join with a mind, then this is how the body will naturally begin to appear. As the Course says, it "will at length be seen as little more than just a shadow circling round the good" (T-31.VII.3:3).

In the end, the Course says, to see someone defined by his body is *incompatible* with seeing him as sinless, which is the way in which we achieve the goal of our relationship. "It *is* impossible to see your brother as sinless and yet to look upon him as a body" (T-20.VII.4:1). Why is this? Is the body inherently sinful? No, the Course says; the body is not good or bad. It is merely neutral, an instrument.

However, the Course says that the body was dreamt up by the mind as physical proof of our illusory separation from God, as a barrier to keep our minds separate from all else. And since deep in our minds we see our separation from God as the original sin, we associate the body with sin. This is all very unconscious, for we do not consciously remember either separating from God or dreaming up the body.

Yet even on the conscious level we can see the implications of viewing someone as a mind walled off from the rest of the world by the body. By walling him off, the body pits him against everything else. It makes him an enemy of the whole, who can only satisfy his needs by scavenging from the whole. The body seems to set this in motion not only by being a boundary, a wall; this wall also has enormous needs of its own, which can only be satisfied through further attack upon the whole. And, to cap it off, the body becomes the instrument of this attack. It becomes "the engine of destruction" (T-20.VIII.4:8), by which we plunder the treasure house of the world around us to feed our separate needs.

Therefore, if we see someone as a body, as a mind contained within a wall of flesh, she will appear to be a walking attack on the whole, an enemy of reality at large, a sinner. Therefore, no matter how challenging it may seem to overlook the body of our partner, for the sake of achieving the goal of our relationship, we must be at least willing to walk in that direction. For this is what allows the means (Christ's vision) to be given us. "The sight that sees the body has no use which serves the purpose of a holy relationship. And while you look upon your brother thus, the means and end have not been brought in line" (T-20.V.5:4-5). We must, then, be willing to have revealed to us a light beyond the body, a holiness beyond form and appearance. For this is who our partner really is. We are not in relationship with a body, but with a spirit that cannot be seen nor touched, but which can be loved.

Your question should not be, "How can I see my brother without the body?" Ask only, "Do I really wish to see him sinless?" And as you ask, forget not that his sinlessness is your escape from fear....Be willing, then, to see your brother sinless, that Christ may rise before your vision and give you joy. And place no value on your brother's body, which holds him to illusions of what he is (T-20.VII.9:1-3,VIII.3:3-4).

~5~
An Exercise in Forgiving Our Savior

A s we said in the last chapter, the entire journey of the holy relationship lies in forgiving each other. And we will have plenty to forgive. In fact, forgiving our holy partner may be the hardest thing we ever do. Why? Because this person, perhaps more than anyone else, has seemingly wounded us, heart and soul. She stirred to life all of our most sacred longings for true fulfillment, and then (according to our version) dashed them against the rocks. Inevitably we compile a long list of the ways in which she has failed our holy venture. True, we have made mistakes along the way, but she has really blown it. The brunt of our joint failure is clearly on her head. She may thus become the supreme symbol for all the ones who "did us wrong." If we can forgive her, we can forgive *anyone*.

Yet how do we forgive her? This is a vast topic, which is really a book unto itself, and that book, you could say, is *A Course in Miracles*. It is an educational program in forgiveness. Hence, if you want to learn how to forgive, do the Course. Approach it as a literal handbook in attaining true forgiveness.

I would, however, like to offer something a bit more specific than this. In forgiving a holy relationship partner I have found it helpful to do an extended forgiveness process that is a kind of combination of Text study and Workbook practice. I have taken passages from the Course and laid them out in such a way that I can treat them like Workbook exercises. There are many, many ways to find forgiveness in a relationship. This is simply one of them.

Our partner as our savior

The passages are focused around the idea of my holy relationship partner being my savior. So before I present the passages, it might help to give a little conceptual background on the concept of savior.

All of us are hoping, in one form or another, that people will save us. That, after all, is what the special relationship is all about. We hope to find that special someone who will save us from our low self-esteem and all our unhappiness. When we join with another in a holy relationship, this hope, rather than going away, probably becomes intensified. Now, we assume, here is someone who is ordained by God to save us. Usually, however, we define this salvation in our way, not in God's.

Inevitably, our partner does not save us as we wished. To put it in more common parlance, she does not meet our needs. Over the course of a lifetime we have accumulated a yawning pit inside of us filled with gaping needs, the (sometimes) hidden content of which is specialness. These needs have been waiting, pining, for the perfect person to come along and finally satiate them. Yet even when we have found that person, she refuses to carry out her (presumed) God-given function and fill our needs. So, of course, we begin to nurse a burning resentment deep in our hearts. Rather than our savior, we come to see her as our executioner.

Forgiveness is only possible when we realize that we have gotten the savior concept completely wrong. We must realize that she was not divinely ordained to save us in the way we thought. One of the most transformative things we can see, I believe, is that it is not her lack of meeting our needs that makes us unhappy, but rather the *needs themselves*. How can the needs themselves possibly make us unhappy? Because when we look to someone to fill our needs, we are in a "getting" mode. We are trying to get, to take from someone, and this affirms that we are lacking, in need, and affirms that we are guilty of the "sin" of taking. Quite simply, it causes us to dislike ourselves. This also blocks our true function of giving, thus cutting off the source of our happiness. I have found it extremely helpful, therefore, to respond to the thoughts of resentment that I catch with the reminder that the other person did not cause my unhappiness; I caused it by being in the getting mode rather than the extension mode. I often use a line from the Course (T-31.III.1:5), changed to read in the first person:

I never hate my brother for his sins, but only for my own.

I blame him for the sin of making me unhappy, but I made me unhappy through the "sin" of trying to get from him. I am blaming him not for his sins, but for mine.

How, then, does our holy relationship partner save us? This, I believe, is crucial to understand. Our holy partner does not save us by filling our needs, but by simply being Who she really is. In truth she is not at all who we thought, but is a completely different person. While we thought we were talking to a human being with a certain name and history, we did not realize that our partner is actually an infinite spiritual being that simply has amnesia. She has forgotten who she is and has acquired the delusion that she is a tiny human.

Our body's eyes see this false her. But we have eyes in us, the eyes of Christ, that can see her as she really is, and the mere sight of her magnitude and shining holiness saves us. How? Because seeing her true nature is an experience of divinity, and such an experience is salvific. Yet this divinity is not simply a beautiful object that we gaze on, for while we are looking on it, *it* is looking upon *us*. When we behold the Christ in her, we see that Christ beholding us, shining on us. And one glance from the eyes of Christ can save us. For what do you think Christ sees in us? His glance saves us because He sees only the *perfect* in us. By seeing us as pure holiness, Christ saves us from our sinful picture of ourselves.

All of this has nothing to do with how our partner sees us consciously or treats us behaviorally. Remember, she saves us merely by our sight of Who she really is, and chances are that she is unaware of her true nature. Yet when we truly see her as she is, we awaken her. She becomes conscious of the Christ in her. The eyes of Christ in her open up and she consciously looks out through those eyes and sees Who *we* really are. And then in her eyes, her words, her gestures and her behavior, we *visibly* experience Christ looking upon us and pronouncing us absolved.

The process, then, is one in which we withdraw our notion of how she was to save us—by meeting our needs, by making us feel special. We lay aside the getting mode and focus on seeing the holiness in her and giving her the acknowledgment of that holiness. Seeing her holiness saves us, and it also saves her. This frees her to actively and consciously take on her role as our savior. The Course has many images of releasing our savior from sleep, from prison, from darkness, from the cross, so that he is now free to save us. "For by this gift is given you the power to release your savior, that he may give salvation unto you" (T-21.II.3:8).

The exercise

The point of the following passages is to treat them as a spiritual practice. The following are the components of doing that:

- Apply every line very specifically to someone in your life, a holy relationship partner if you have one. You can, however, use this exercise for anyone. Hold that person in mind and occasionally insert his or her name.
- Apply the "you" to yourself. You may even want to change the passages into first person, changing "you" into "I."
- Approach each line with all of your mind. Read it slowly, dwell on it. Make it real for you. Spend some time with it.
- Do not let any line be empty. Do not go on to the next line until this line has sunk in at least a little.
- Imagine that each line is really true. If your mind resists its truth, simply entertain the possibility that it is true.
- Think of specific examples where applicable.
- Visualize the imagery, see the action.
- Feel free to elaborate on the lines and thereby make them more personal.

If, in going through this once you find that it works for you, you may want to make an extended forgiveness process of it. Go through it as often as you can, ideally every day, for as long as it takes—until you have reached the perception of the other person that you want. During the day when you are not doing the exercise, watch your thoughts about this person. Whenever you notice a resentful or judgmental thought, respond with one of the ideas from here that you have found useful. And if it takes you a year of daily practice, it will probably be the best year you have ever spent.

In the following, I have not changed any of the wording from the Course. I have edited out certain lines for the sake of flow, but have indicated that with ellipses. References are found at the end of a passage, not at the end of each piece of it.

The first passage is from Workbook Lesson 78. It is an actual exercise from the Course. You begin by holding someone in mind, in this case a holy relationship partner. In reviewing how you now consider this person, I suggest you take each line separately.

You will attempt to hold him in your mind, first as you now consider him.

You will review his faults [think of a couple examples],

the difficulties you have had with him [a few examples],

the pain he caused you [examples],

his neglect,

and all the little and the larger hurts he gave.

You will regard his body

with its flaws and better points as well,

and you will think of his mistakes and even of his "sins."

Earlier in this lesson our mass of grievances is called a "dark shield of hate." On that shield is depicted what we just reviewed: this person's body and all the wrong that body has apparently done us. Now we can see ourselves setting this shield down and lifting our eyes in faith, as we ask the Holy Spirit to show us the light beyond the dark shield.

Then let us ask of Him [the Holy Spirit] Who knows this Son of God in his reality and truth,

that we may look on him a different way,

and see our savior shining in the light of true forgiveness, given unto us [visualize this].

We ask Him in the holy Name of God and of His Son, as holy as Himself:

Let me behold my savior in this one
You have appointed as the one for me
to ask to lead me to the holy light
in which he stands, that I may join with him.

Use this prayer repeatedly, each time thinking deeply about its meaning, each time letting its meaning sink in more deeply. You are asking to behold this person as your savior. Let us not water down that word "savior." A savior is someone so holy that their simple glance can heal you in mind and body. You are acknowledging that the Holy Spirit has specifically appointed this person as the one you will ask for salvation. What a holy request!

Visualize the final phrases. See this person taking you by the hand and gently leading you into the holy light in which they stand, in which they abide. See yourself now standing there with them, light now bathing both of you, shining from both of you, and then see the two of you uniting in light.

> The body's eyes are closed, and as you think of him who grieved you,
> let your mind be shown the light in him beyond your grievances [beyond the dark shield of hate]....
> The Holy Spirit leans from him to you, seeing no separation in God's Son [feel the Holy Spirit leaning from them to you].
> And what you see through Him will free you both [feel the freedom].
> Be very quiet now, and look upon your shining savior [see the Great Rays radiating out from them].
> No dark grievances obscure the sight of him [the shield has been thrown aside].
> You have allowed the Holy Spirit to express through him the role [of savior] God gave Him that you might be saved. (W-pI.78.6-8)

Did you notice how we dispel our dark memories of all the hurt, difficulty, grief and neglect we received from this person? Did we express our rage and get it out of our system? Did we have to work anything out with the person, come to any understandings? Did we have to understand why they did what they did or come to some kinder explanation of what motivated them? No, all we did was answer our grievances with the light. We simply set two views of this person next to each other. The one view sees them as a body that has done us harm. The other view sees them as a shining spirit that can lead us home. We simply set these views side by side and let the light dispel the darkness.

What follows is a virtually identical exercise, this one from Lesson 161. Again we begin by reviewing our partner's apparent identity.

> Select one brother, symbol of the rest, and ask salvation of him.
> See him first as clearly as you can [really visualize what follows, point-by-point],

in that same form to which you are accustomed.
See his face,
his hands and feet,
his clothing.
Watch him smile,
and see familiar gestures which he makes so frequently.
Then think of this [really think and ponder on this]:
What you are seeing now conceals from you
the sight of one who can forgive you all your sins;
whose sacred hands can take away the nails which pierce
your own,
and lift the crown of thorns which you have placed upon
your bleeding head.

Really picture these last two things. The Course says, "You have nailed yourself to a cross, and placed a crown of thorns upon your own head" (T-11.VI.8:1). The image, then, is that you are on the cross, put there by yourself. Realize that this is a symbol for the fact that you do feel crucified, that you feel bound, trapped, punished, persecuted, limited by many things, but ultimately by your own "sins." See your savior approaching you, shining in light. See and feel their "sacred hands" removing the nails that fix you to the cross. See and feel them lifting the crown of thorns from your head. Realize that this person has the power to take you down from the cross, just by being Who they really are.

Ask this of him, that he may set you free:
Give me your blessing, holy Son of God.
I would behold you with the eyes of Christ,
and see my perfect sinlessness in you.

Again, pray this prayer many times, letting your mind take in the meaning of each word. If this person really is a divine being, the Son of God, what more valuable treasure could you have than their *blessing*? Their blessing would grant you pure blessedness. It would be salvation. And if only you could look upon them through the eyes of Christ, you would see that they *are* the Son of God. And you *want* to see them through these eyes:

"I *would* behold you...." The eyes of Christ in you would reveal standing before you a perfectly sinless Being, Who sees perfect sinlessness in you, and Whose blessing lets you see it, too.

> And He will answer Whom you called upon [the light in their mind will answer you, regardless of their conscious knowledge of your request].
>
> For He will hear the Voice for God in you [in your request for blessing], and answer in your own [voice].
>
> Behold him now, whom you have seen as merely flesh and bone,
>
> and recognize that Christ has come to you.
> (W-pI.161.11-12)

That final line is very powerful. The phrase, "whom you have seen as merely flesh and bone," refers to that initial review of how you see this person, as face, hands, feet, clothing, expressions and gestures, and also as the personality you deduce from all of these added together. Realize you have been totally mistaken about who this person is. This is no insignificant pile of moving meat. This is Christ Himself. How would you feel if you really believed that Christ had come to you? In the guise of this person?

Notice that in this exercise, like in Lesson 78, the darkness is not *dealt with*. It is merely called to mind and answered with the light. We get in touch with our current (faulty) view of this person, and then dispel it with the realization that they are our savior.

As you do these exercises remember to dwell on every line. Drink in every line. It will help to occasionally insert the person's name. The following two exercises do this for you. Notice the effect of inserting the name. In these exercises I find it helps to visualize the light. Even though the light referred to here is not physical, visible light, such light can serve as a good symbol for the non-physical light of holiness.

> *You stand with me in light, [name].*
> (W-pI.rII.87. 2:3)

> *The light in you is all that I would see,* [name].
> (W-pI.rII.88. 2:3)

In this latter exercise, try visualizing the Great Rays pouring off of this person, shining out into infinity. Affirm that those Rays are all you want to see in that person.

The following passage is from the closing part of "The Obstacles to Peace," which we will discuss in Chapter 7.

> Beside you is one who offers you the chalice of Atonement,
> for the Holy Spirit is in him.

Again, really visualize this. See this person approach you, filled with the Holy Spirit, shining with holiness. See their hands holding out the Holy Grail to you. Take the cup from their hands, lift it to your lips and drink in the Atonement. Feel the wine of Atonement absolving you of all guilt, liberating you from all limitation. Imagine how thankful you would be for the hands that gave you this indescribable gift.

> Would you hold his sins against him, or accept his gift to you?...
> He has in him the power to forgive your sin, as you for him....
> Let him be what he is, and seek not to make of love an enemy.

> Behold your Friend, the Christ Who stands beside you [how would you feel if you really believed this?].
> How holy and how beautiful He is!
> You thought He sinned because you cast the veil of sin upon Him to hide His loveliness.
> Yet still He holds forgiveness out to you, to share His holiness.
> This "enemy," this "stranger" still offers you salvation as His Friend....

I visualize the above lines in terms of the veil over the face of Christ. Looming right behind my partner's body I imagine a massive radiant face, the face of love, the face of Christ, "shining with joy because

He is in His Father's Love" (T-19.IV(D).2:2). And then I visualize my current picture of my partner—as a body that sins—as an image on a cloth veil hanging in front of this face. I realize that I cast this veil upon this shining face of my own free will, in order to hide the intense loveliness of the face. "Yet still"—yet even then He offers me His holiness as His Friend.

> This [Friend, this Christ] is your brother, [name], crucified
> by sin and waiting for release from pain.

Imagine that the picture on the veil becomes a picture of your partner's body nailed to a cross. Then imagine the immense face behind the veil with His eyes closed, as He painfully dreams that He *is* this body "crucified by sin and waiting for release from pain."

> Would you not offer him forgiveness, when only he can
> offer it to you [ask yourself this]?
> For his redemption he will give you yours [is it worth it?],
> as surely as God created every living thing and loves it....
> There is no grace of Heaven that you cannot offer to your
> brother, [name],
> and receive from your most holy Friend....
> Forgive the sins your brother thinks he has committed,
> and all the guilt you think you see in him.

> Think who your brother [name] is, before you would
> condemn him [really think on this].
> And offer thanks to God that he is holy [actually offer this
> thanks],
> and has been given the gift of holiness for you [could any
> gift be more desirable?].
> Join him in gladness,
> and remove all trace of guilt from his disturbed and
> tortured mind.
> Help him to lift the heavy burden of sin you laid upon him
> and he accepted as his own,
> and toss it lightly and with happy laughter away from him.

Press it not like thorns against his brow,
nor nail him to it, unredeemed and hopeless.
(T-19.IV(D).12,13,14,15,16,17)

For these last lines picture yourself walking up to the veil on which your partner's crucified body is. Symbolically lift from them all of the sins that you laid on them and that they laid on themselves. You may picture it as lifting an iron crown of thorns from their head. You may picture it as lifting a cross they are carrying. You may picture it as throwing aside the veil entirely. Either way, realize that you are freeing the beautiful face from its long nightmare of sin and crucifixion.

> You *have* the vision that enables you to see the body not.
> And as you look upon your brother [name], you will see an altar to your Father,
> holy as Heaven, glowing with radiant purity
> and sparkling with the shining lilies you laid upon it.
> (T-20.VIII. 4:3-4; emphasis mine)

As you picture your partner, look past their body as if it were transparent. Just past where the body used to be, imagine a wide circle of light, in the center of which is an altar to God, made of gleaming marble and "glowing with radiant purity." This altar is a symbol of who your partner really is. It signifies that at their core lies nothing but pure and holy devotion to God, total and innocent acknowledgment of their Creator. An altar to God is who they are. See yourself walking up and placing a gift on their altar, in honor of what it is. Your gift is white lilies of forgiveness. This is your gesture of absolving them for all you thought they did, affirming that all their sins were illusion. Placing this gift on their altar is your acknowledgment of the holiness they really are and of the Holy One Who created this altar to Himself. See the lilies begin to glow and shine like the rest of the altar.

> Here stands your brother [name] with the key to Heaven in his hand, held out to you.
> Let not the dream of specialness remain between you.
> (T-24.II.7:6-7)

Again, actually visualize this scene. See your partner standing before you, offering you the key to Heaven, waiting for you to take it. What would you rather have than this key? For, one turn of this key and you are in peace eternal. What blocks your acceptance of this key is your dream of being special, and your thought that your partner's real function is to satisfy your need to feel special.

> The key you threw away God gave your brother, [name],
> whose holy hands would offer it to you
> when you were ready to accept His plan for your salvation
> in the place of yours.
> (T-24.II.14:1)

The "key" in this passage, by the way, is the key to the gate of Heaven *and* the key *out of* "the gates of hell you closed upon yourself" (this is the sentence right before the passage). In other words, you locked yourself in hell and threw away the key! Picture this scene in your mind, in whatever form you wish. Then picture God taking the key you threw away and giving it to your partner. Picture their "holy hands" offering it to you—when you accept that you will be saved by seeing their holiness, rather than seeing their sinfulness.

> He [the Holy Spirit] stands beside the door to which
> forgiveness is the only key.
> Give it to Him to use instead of you,
> and you will see the door swing silently open upon the
> shining face of Christ.
> Behold your brother [name] there beyond the door;
> the Son of God as He created him.
> (S-2.III.7:6-8)

The context for this passage is that we do not understand forgiveness as the unconditional release it really is. Therefore we must let the Holy Spirit forgive through us. That is what giving Him the key means. Visualize giving Him this key. I further suggest you visualize an image of your partner painted or projected on the door, so that the opening of the door symbolizes the removal of your false image of them. As the door opens you see "the shining face of Christ" filling the doorway. You behold this face in wonder and realize This is Who your partner really is.

> Before your brother's holiness the world is still,
> and peace descends on it in gentleness and blessing so complete
> that not one trace of conflict still remains
> to haunt you in the darkness of the night....

I find this sentence to be breathtaking. First imagine a scene in which the world is locked in mindless conflict in a dark night. You might want to read the description of conflict in "the dark forest of the sightless" in the previous section (T-24.V.4). Then your partner's holiness appears, visualized as a radiant circle of light, or as the glowing face of Christ, or as a Christ-figure in shining robes, or however. Suddenly, all conflict ceases and the entire world falls still as it gazes on their holiness. And as it gazes, peace comes over the enchanted masses. And peace comes over you, too, dispelling all trace of conflict that has haunted you "in the darkness of the night." Such is the holiness of this sight.

> In him is your assurance God is here, and with you now [realize that God Himself is present within the glowing light of your partner's holiness].
> While he is what he is, you can be sure that God is knowable
> and will be known to you [take this statement in].
> For He could never leave His Own creation.
> And the sign that this is so lies in your brother, [name],
> offered you that all your doubts about yourself [call to mind some of those doubts]
> may disappear before his holiness.
> (T-24.VI.1)

This last sentence is remarkable. The proof that God could never leave you lies in your partner's holiness. This proof, this presence of God in your partner, is offered you so that, as you gaze on their holiness, all doubts you ever had about yourself will vanish. You will doubt yourself no more.

You will know God is with you. You will know Who you are.

There are many more passages we could lay out like this. Part of the function of this chapter, though, was to simply give you a way to read the holy relationship sections in the Text. If you are truly serious about forgiving your holy relationship partner, you might want to go through Chapters 17 through 22 in a similar to what we have done here, reading them as directly applying to your relationship.

To review the main concepts behind this practice:

- Your partner is someone else entirely than who you thought they were.
- Their holiness has power to save you, merely by you beholding it, and seeing it behold you. This has nothing to do with their conscious attitudes or behavior toward you.
- Seeing their holiness not only saves you. It saves them and sets them free to actively, consciously return the gift to you.

This will take practice. If you really want to forgive your partner, be willing to practice until the miracle comes. Expect the miracle, claim your right to it, and do not give up practicing until you experience it.

~*6*~
A Common State of Mind

A ll of the methods we have just discussed seem to be geared toward individual application. And in the holy relationship individual application remains extremely important. Yet the meaning of the holy relationship lies in oneness. The exercises done by yourself are a way of bringing to your mind the awareness of oneness with your partner, the oneness of goal and the oneness of Self. In this chapter we will explore the practical implications of oneness.

Recall our discussion from Chapter 1, in which we said that the significance of sharing a common purpose was that it brought our minds together: "those who share a purpose have a mind as one" (T-IV.7:4). Sharing a single goal unites our minds in a common experience, the experience of valuing, desiring and pursuing that goal. It puts our minds in the same state. As the Course says, "reason sees a holy relationship as what it is; a common state of mind..." (T-22.III.9:7).

What does it mean to have a common state of mind? In the following three points we will explore the implications of having a common state and how we can use that toward our goal.

1. Whatever one experiences, the other will experience with him

Your common purpose has opened a link between your minds. That link has always been there, for in reality your minds are one. But your holy union, which your common purpose invited into your relationship, has now made that link operative in your conscious experience. What this means is that your minds begin to operate as one. On some deep level they fall in step with each other. They begin to go through the same phases, have the same realizations, work on the same lessons, chew on the same issues. Not that differences will be obliterated. But when you talk together about what has really been going on inside of each of you, you will often detect strikingly common threads. You will find that one of you began to go through a certain phase at almost the same time that the other began a very similar phase. This is evidence of the single plan that now unites your lives, welding your two paths to God into a single journey.

This also means that whenever one of you experiences anger, fear or any sort of ego attack, it is a threat to both, which both will experience. And not just because the angry one will draw the other into an argument. Even before that happens an exchange will have taken place on the mind level. And the ensuing argument will just obscure the inner fact that now you both are in this together.

> But forget not that your relationship is one, and so it must be that whatever threatens the peace of one is an equal threat to the other. The power of joining its blessing lies in the fact that it is now impossible for you or your brother to experience fear alone, or to attempt to deal with it alone. Never believe that this is necessary, or even possible (T-18.V.6:3-5).

The temptation is to see this as a burden: "Oh, great. Now when I feel bad I have to feel guilty for causing her to feel bad. And when I feel good I have to worry about her dragging me down." Yet the Course urges us, "Look not with fear upon this happy fact, and think not that it lays a heavy burden on you....Do not attempt to keep a little of the ego with this gift" (T-22.VI.14:4,15:4). Instead, we are told to look to the positive implications: "Would you regret you cannot fear alone when your relationship can also teach the power of love is there, which makes all fear impossible?" (T-22.VI.15:3)

The exact nature of these positive implications will be discussed in the next two points.

2. Either one of you—it does not matter which one—has the power to save both

The obvious implication of the fact that "what one thinks, the other will experience with him" (T-22.VI.14:2), is the fact that each one has the power, not only to depress both, but also to *release* both. We discussed this in Chapter 4 under the heading of ACIM conflict resolution. Here is a portion of that passage which we have not yet looked at:

...it is now impossible for you or your brother to experience fear alone....Yet just as this is impossible, so is it equally impossible that the holy instant come to either of you without the other. And it will come to both at the request of either.

Whoever is saner at the time the threat is perceived should remember how deep is his indebtedness to the other and how much gratitude is due him, and be glad that he can pay his debt by bringing happiness to both [by accepting a holy instant for both] (T-18.V.6:4-7:1).

One aspect of this idea, which is already visible in the above passage, is that it really does not matter who does the releasing. Since you are both one, focusing on who made the healing possible is like asking which hand opened the door, the right or the left. This is true, we are told, in the context of two people joined together in prayer:

Perhaps the specific form of resolution for a specific problem will occur to either of you; it does not matter which. Perhaps it will reach both, if you are genuinely attuned to one another. It will come because you have realized that Christ is in both of you. That is its only truth (S-1.I.7:8-11).

It is even true in the context of psychotherapy, in which the therapist, not the patient, is the one who is expected to provide the initial willingness for healing: "The willingness may come from either one at the beginning, and as the other shares it, it will grow" (P-2.III.2:5).

3. Your union has the power to dispel the ego and reveal God

The implication of oneness that gets by far the most press in the Course is that the very fact of our union gives us the power to overlook the ego and also becomes our lamp that reveals God. There are many ways in which the Course tells us this.

We are told that because we experience the same state of mind in the holy relationship, this proves that we must be the same. "Here is belief in differences undone. Here is the faith in differences shifted to sameness" (T-Intro.4:2-3). This has the further effect of proving that, despite appearances, we cannot really attack each other. How could we? We are one. Can a finger attack itself? It must only be our belief in differences that conjures up the illusion that we can attack each other. For the oneness we are now experiencing proves that in reality we cannot.

Further, our oneness gives us the perfect opportunity to overlook the ego. By ourselves, the ego must seem forever real. For the ego is the belief that we *are* by ourselves. And so looking at it on our own is looking at it from its vantage point. It is like using your hands to feel your body and then based on their evidence concluding that the body is real.

Think what joining does to our ego's sense of reality and solidity. I may be totally convinced that I am just me, that I am this little ball of arms and legs, tissue and bones, thoughts, feelings, memories and goals. I may be convinced that in the end no one else belongs in here but me. Yet when I join with another person I experience something very real, yet something that is, in the end, totally incompatible with my belief in being a solitary ego.

Now I have to choose. Which one am I? Am I the being that exists in total isolation? Am I the island that I thought I was? Or am I the being that joined? Does my real identity actually include the other person?

If you and I decide to commit ourselves to the latter, then we have a very powerful tool with which to dispel my belief in separate identity. We just need to look at my sense of separate selfhood from the vantage point of our union. We look at all my little fears and resentments, my need to control and my desire for specialness, from the perspective of our oneness. And from that vantage point my ego will look totally different than it looks from the inside. It will look false. After all these years, I will realize that I am not who I thought I was at all.

> For no one alone can judge the ego truly. Yet when two or more join together in searching for truth, the ego can no longer defend its lack of content. The fact of union tells them it is not true (T-14.X.9:5-7).

> Look gently on your brother, and remember the ego's weakness is revealed in both your sight. What it would keep apart has met and joined, and looks upon the ego unafraid (T-21.IV.8:1-2).

And so, our most powerful tool in the holy relationship is our togetherness. Individual application of truth is extremely valuable, yet this will lead to the experience of joining, which in the end is the real power in the holy relationship. When our seemingly separate minds join and look on things together, it will be as if we have put on magic glasses (or perhaps I should say "miracle glasses"). Whatever we look upon will be revealed for what it is. If we look on the false, it will look false; it will seem small, inconsequential, unnecessary. If we look on the true, it will leap to our gaze as vibrant and real. As the Course says, "If you undertake the search together, you bring with you a light so powerful that what you see is given meaning" (T-14.X.10:6).

In fact, we are told that only by journeying together will we reach the last obstacle to peace, the veil that hangs before the face of Christ: the fear of God. And we will only surmount this last obstacle by doing so together. It is to this place that our original moment of joining has led us, and only through joining will we pass beyond it. "Together we will disappear into the Presence beyond the veil, not to be lost but found; not to be seen but known" (T-19.IV(D).19:1).

> No one can stand before this obstacle alone, for he could not have reached this far unless his brother walked beside him....And so you and your brother stand, here in this holy place, before the veil of sin that hangs between you and the face of Christ. Let it be lifted! Raise it together with your brother, for it is but a veil that stands between you. Either you or your brother alone will see it as a solid block, nor realize how thin the drapery that separates you now (T-19.IV(D).4:2, T-22.IV.3:1-4).

Thus, in the end, we do get back to God together. I remember several years ago having a discussion with a friend about relationships. He punctuated his point with something like the following question, which was meant to be rhetorical: "When you finish your journey back to God, and you are making your final ascent, who is going to be there with you?" The answer was simply assumed to be "no one." This was supposed to show that we should not get too into people here (or something along those lines), for when it is all said and done, we return to God alone. Well, what my friend and I only realized some time later was that in fact this is not what the Course is saying. On its path, we really do enter the ark of peace two by two.

It is impossible to remember God in secret and alone. For remembering Him means you are not alone....The lonely journey fails because it has excluded what it would find (T-14.X.10:1-2,7).

~7~
Reaching the Goal of Holiness

A s we saw in the first chapter of Part II, the holy relationship is a process. It "begins, develops and becomes accomplished" (T-17.V.2:4). As such, the initial period of discomfort will most likely last a good while, perhaps many years. In other words, do not feel like you are a miserable failure if after ten years, or even twenty years, you still have not reached a place of deep, genuine serenity together. Give it time, and especially keep giving it your willingness, no matter what else happens.

But, unless one or both of you gives up (which simply postpones things), then you will slowly pull out of the period of discomfort. Things will get gradually brighter. As the Course says about the initial change of purpose, "As this change develops and is finally accomplished, it becomes increasingly beneficent and joyous" (T-17.V.5:3). In this chapter, we will look at some of the characteristics of the maturing holy relationship.

Each becomes the other's savior

In Chapter 5 we discussed the whole idea of being each other's saviors. This notion is a subtle and sophisticated idea. But, to put it briefly, we save another by seeing the holiness in her. Her holiness saves us without her conscious cooperation. It saves us just by being what it is, just by shining its light on us and pronouncing us holy. However, by our truly seeing it in her we save her, and thus we set her free to actively and consciously save us in return.

This is what begins to happen in a maturing holy relationship. Each one begins to take on his function of savior of the other. Each one starts to really see that saving the other is his own salvation. In short, each one begins to care for the other as if the other were himself.

Every mistake you and your brother make, the other will

gently have corrected for you. For in his sight your loveliness is his salvation, which he would protect from harm. And each will be the other's strong protector from everything that seems to rise between you (T-22.IV.5:1-3).

This even extends to physical needs. For if the other is really yourself, as in fact she is, nothing should be barred from the relationship. In discussing the issue of the therapist receiving money from the patient, we are told the following:

> If their relationship is to be holy, whatever one needs is given by the other; whatever one lacks the other supplies. Herein is the relationship made holy, for herein both are healed. The therapist repays the patient in gratitude, as does the patient repay him. There is no cost to either. But thanks are due to both, for the release from long imprisonment and doubt (P-3.III.4:4-8).

What this all means is that my function in the relationship is to consistently overlook your ego. No matter how much your ego may act out, no matter how many tantrums it may throw, it is my job to *not* see you as that. And through consistently not seeing you as that I will finally convince you that you are more than that. For you will in large measure live up (or down) to what I think you are.

Giving, not bargaining

Free giving, giving for the joy of giving, is what characterizes the advanced holy relationship. What we call giving usually has a great many hooks and strings attached, especially in our most valued relationships. We looked at this issue in Part I. We think of giving as a sacrifice, and so the only way we can justify doing such a crazy thing is if it can get us something in return, hopefully something of even more value. Our gift is a sacrifice, a voluntary loss for the sake of the other, the actual purpose of which is to allow us to "justifiably" guilt her into giving us something in return.

This is just one of the many ways in which we try to control our partner. For in the unholy relationship the whole point is to get her to treat our ego and our body in the way that we want. And so to this end we give "gifts," we apply pressure, we promise gifts upon the meeting of certain conditions, we blame her, we attack her, we withhold favors. All of these are actually different forms of "motivating" her through guilt or the threat of guilt. We figure that if we dropped this weapon entirely, she would certainly have no reason to treat us right. In fact, she would probably just get up and walk out. The whole idea is to use guilt to hound her into doing our ego's bidding.

One of the most dramatic things about the mature holy relationship is the actual reversal of this way of being. We give for the sake of giving, for the joy of taking care of our savior, in the confidence that this act saves us both. And we leave her end up to her. We trust that she is actually good enough to hold up her end by herself. Instead of trying to control her, to take care of her end for her, we just take care of our own part. And what this means is that we give to her, with no strings attached.

If we understand this reversal, this can allay any fears we have about true joining being just another way to sacrifice what is most true and genuine within us. Because of our experience in special relationships, it is easy for us to fear that for the sake of being joined we will have to stifle ourselves, our values, our qualities, our uniqueness and individuality.

This, of course, is true only of the false joining of the special relationship. There, we *do* need to stifle our individuality—and do what we can to stifle our partner's—in order to hold the relationship together. The reason for this comes down to the actual nature of the joining. For we do not join on the level of our true Self; we do not even join an honest and complete version of our personalities. What we do is hand-pick a few very superficial aspects of the two of us—certain "acceptable" personality traits and certain "desirable" body parts. We then take these "select" parts and meld them together to make an idealized image of who we are as a couple. We construct a fantasy image of our togetherness. And this is what we each unite with. The Course makes this false joining into a very simple lesson in arithmetic:

> When two individuals seek to become one, they are trying to decrease their magnitude....If one such union were made in perfect faith, the universe would enter into it. Yet the special relationship the ego seeks does not include even one whole individual. The ego wants but part of him... (T-16.VI.5:3,6-8).

Because we have joined such superficial aspects of ourselves, the more the two of us reach down inside and express what is really within us—our honest darkness and our authentic light—the more the image we have made is going to be blown apart, and probably the relationship with it; hence, the need to control.

In a holy relationship, the joining takes place at the opposite end of the spectrum. Rather than joining superficial aspects of ourselves, our minds have actually been united at the base, the foundation. Thus, the more each one of us authentically moves from our own inner foundation, the more we will actually benefit the joining. And because of the commitment made in our original holy instant, and the Force which was thus invited into the relationship, both of us can be implicitly trusted to do our part. We do not need to force each other, to bribe each other or to rub each other's noses in anything. We will each do our part of our own free accord.

The holy relationship, then, is about freedom: free giving and free expression. If it is mature, it can handle a great deal of diversity out of its trust in the true depth of the union. As the Course says,

> Love is freedom. To look for it by placing yourself in bondage is to separate yourself from it. For the Love of God, no longer seek for union in separation, nor for freedom in bondage! As you release, so will you be released (T-16.VI.2:1-4).

The gifts of the holy relationship

As we begin to apply all of these perspectives and climb out of the period of discomfort, we will begin to experience the happiness and joy that comes from the holy relationship. The Course implies that it is the most joy we can experience this side of Heaven, for remember, "In this world, God's Son comes closest to himself in a holy relationship" (T-20.V.1:1).

> Think of the loveliness that you will see, who walk with Him! And think how beautiful will you and your brother look to the other! How happy you will be to be together, after such a long and lonely journey where you walked alone (T-22.IV.4:1-3).

> And gladly will you and your brother walk the way of

innocence together, singing as you behold the open door of
Heaven and recognize the home that called to you. Give
joyously to one another the freedom and the strength to
lead you there. And come before each other's holy altar
where the strength and freedom wait, to offer and receive
the bright awareness that leads you home. The lamp is lit
in both of you for one another. And by the hands that gave
it to your brother shall both of you be led past fear to love
(T-20.II.11:3-7).

Several distinct but completely overlapping things will happen.
First, we will begin to see ourselves as whole, as innocent and holy. Second,
we will begin to see our partner as the same as us and one with us. We will
slowly wear away all those boundaries that seemed so real, so important
and so final:

> ...each one learns that giving and receiving are the same.
> The demarcations they have drawn between their roles,
> their minds, their bodies, their needs, their interests, an all
> the differences they thought separated them from one
> another, fade and grow dim and disappear (M-2.5:5-6).

> Think what a holy relationship can teach! Here is
> belief in differences undone. Here is the faith in
> differences shifted to sameness (T-22.IN.4:1-3).

We will also begin to look out together on an innocent world:

> Who in a holy relationship can long remain unholy? The
> world the holy see is one with them, just as the world the
> ego looks upon is like itself. The world the holy see is
> beautiful because they see their innocence in it....They
> gently questioned it and whispered, "What are you?" and
> He Who watches over all perception answered (T-
> 20.III.6:1-3,5-6).

Finally, we will begin to acquire the characteristics of the teacher
of God, which are *trust, honesty, tolerance, gentleness, joy, defenselessness,
generosity, patience, faithfulness and open-mindedness*. I think almost all

Course students are familiar with this list of the characteristics of the teacher of God. What is usually overlooked, however, is the fact that "These special gifts" are "born in the holy relationship" (M-4.1:6).

We have already discussed somewhat the process sketched in the Manual for Teachers: First, someone makes a choice in which he does "not see his interests as apart from someone else's" (M-1.1:2). This choice makes him a teacher of God and his pupils then begin to answer an inner summons and seek him out. Once they find him, he and they "join together for learning purposes" (M-2.5:3); they join in the common goal of learning the same course, the same spiritual path. This invites the Holy Spirit into the relationship. Then, as their holy relationship matures over time and all the boundaries between them "fade and grow dim and disappear" (M-2.5:6), the teacher of God is transformed into an advanced teacher by the holiness of the relationship. It is out of the advanced holy relationship, then, "toward which the teaching-learning situation is geared" (M-4.1:6), that the teacher acquires the ten characteristics of the teacher of God. In this way we can see that the first four sections of the Manual describe a single process through which the teacher of God travels.

Preparation for union with God

The reason that the holy relationship contains so many incredible gifts is that it is actually practice for Heaven. It is preparation for the ultimate holy relationship: our relationship with God. Its oneness is a reflection of the "perfect union and unbroken continuity" (T-20.VI.1:5) of God's oneness with us. This is why the Course says of the person in a holy relationship:

> Just under Heaven does he stand, but close enough not to return to earth. For this relationship has Heaven's holiness. How far from home can a relationship so like to Heaven be? (T-22.IN.3:2-9)

And this is why it says of the holy relationship itself:

> ...Heaven has come to earth at last, from which the ego's rule has kept it out so long. Heaven has come because it found a home in your relationship on earth. And earth can hold no longer what has been given Heaven as its own (T-21.IV.7:5-7).

To me, this is perhaps the most important thing about the holy relationship; that in it we are learning how to be in union with God. Being in relationship with each other is like being at the gym training for the Olympics. Someday the work we have done together will have prepared us for the ultimate relationship. And at that point our oneness will flower into something far greater, into oneness with all of reality and with its Creator, our Father.

Lifting the veil

The section called "The Obstacles to Peace," the longest and perhaps most important section in the Text, is really about the holy relationship. Course students do not seem to generally recognize this, yet this section paints a powerful portrait of the holy relationship's journey toward its goal. The reason this is not often seen is that the connective tissue that knits the section together is subtle and hard to detect. So I would like to present a brief description here of that tissue as I understand it.

When you and your brother joined in a holy instant the Holy Spirit's peace (elsewhere spoken of as His goal of holiness) was placed deep within the relationship. The natural motion of this peace is to flow out and surround you and your brother in peace, and then flow out to the world and encompass everyone in peace. When this is done, the Holy Spirit's purpose will be done, and God will take the final step.

The ego, of course, does not want peace. It will do everything it can to throw up obstacles to this "invasion" of peace. For it is actually *attracted* to guilt, pain, fear and death (as we are told in various parts of this section). Its core commitment is to the goal of sin, and so it wants to prove that sin is real by giving sin various "real" results (guilt, punishment, fear, death).

In the holy instant that began the holy relationship, the Holy Spirit's peace entered at a very deep level of mind. At this level, peace replaced your belief in sin. This means that the deep foundation of your belief in sin was wiped away. Your belief in sin was "uprooted," so to speak. With its foundation gone, there remains only a microscopic remnant of your belief in sin; tiny and unstable.

This tiny remnant of the belief in sin, however, still tries to preserve itself. It does so by placing obstacles before the flow of peace. The obstacles are not merely a series or a collection, but are like chinese boxes, each nested inside the other. Each obstacle exists as a protection for the one following it, and is *produced* by the one following it for that very protection. It stands in front so that the next one is shielded from being exposed and removed. It accomplishes this by lying. Each obstacle is a lie, which protects the deeper lie that comes after it. This means that the more you travel through the obstacles, the deeper you travel into the ego's unconscious depths, into its core lie. This also means that all the obstacles are generated by, and exist to protect, the final obstacle: the fear of God.

The first three obstacles are thus a system of defense, a series of protections, for the fear of God. The body is at the center of this system. It is what ties the first three obstacles together: its pleasure, its pain, its punishment and its death. On the surface, we fear the Holy Spirit's peace (the first obstacle) because of our attraction to physical pleasure (the second obstacle). Yet our attraction to pleasure is not an attraction to happiness but at root an attraction to guilt, pain and finally to death (the third obstacle). And this attraction to death comes from our fear of God's Life (the final obstacle).

Peace will inevitably flow over the obstacles, for the belief in sin is now only a powerless, tiny feather. And in the end you are more attracted to peace than to sin, guilt, pain, fear and death. Peace will first flow over the most superficial obstacle and slowly wend its way down to the final obstacle, the fear of God.

And here, before the final obstacle, the Course sketches a dramatic picture. You and your brother stand a step away from the end of the journey. You stand together in front of the veil before the face of Christ. The veil is the fear of God, the fear of God's Love, of disappearing into His unlimited Life and losing all separate identity. All you need do is look upon this veil, see that it is nothing and let it be lifted. But you are terrified to look up, fearing the permanent loss of your ego and your world.

There is only one way to overcome this terror, says the Course:

> But first, lift up your eyes and look on your brother in innocence born of complete forgiveness of his illusions, and through the eyes of faith that sees them not....No one can stand before this obstacle alone, for he could not have reached this far unless his brother walked beside him. And no one would dare to look on it without complete forgiveness of his brother in his heart (T-19.IV(D).8:7-9:3).

The way beyond the final veil is to forgive your brother and receive forgiveness from him. Each of you must be savior to the other, giving and receiving the same gift of release from guilt. Each of you must be willing to take the nails out of the other's hands, lift the crown of thorns from his head, and look upon the Christ in him.

By doing this you will be ready to lift the veil. Indeed, by doing this you *will* be lifting the veil. For it is a veil that covers the face of Christ, that blocks the vision of the true Self in each of you. Therefore, while you fail to realize that your brother *is* the Christ, you have obscured your sight of him. You have veiled him. The veil stands not only before the two of you, but *between* you.

> Raise it together with your brother, for it is but a veil that stands between you. Either you or your brother alone will see it as a solid block, nor realize how thin the drapery that separates you now (T-22.IV.3:3-4).

By forgiving each other, then, the two of you lift the veil, as if uncovering the face of a bride. And together you look upon the face of Christ, blazing with "the bright rays of His Father's Love that light His face with glory" (T-19.IV(D).2:3). This poetic image means that together you see with vision and look on the shining presence of Christ in everyone and everything. And having achieved the means of your relationship's goal—the means being vision—you will achieve the goal itself: *salvation*. The two of you will be lifted up and resurrected beyond the veil, past the face of Christ to unite with the Christ Himself, and there to remember God.

> Together we will disappear into the Presence beyond the veil, not to be lost but found; not to be seen but known. And knowing, nothing in the plan God has established for salvation will be left undone. This is the journey's purpose [its goal], without which is the journey meaningless. Here is the peace of God, given to you eternally by Him. Here is the rest and quiet that you seek, the reason for the journey from its beginning (T-19.IV(D).19:1-5).

In summary, through forgiving your holy relationship partner, you will be confronting the absolute core of your ego, facing the primordial terror that has kept you in solitary misery for untold eons. And through that same forgiveness you will achieve Christ's vision and reach the end of the spiritual journey. Through your holy relationship you will find salvation from the human condition.

~8~
Our Joint Special Function

Yet before you disappear forever beyond the veil, there is one thing left that you must do. You must return to this world and give it the gift that you have received.

Think what will happen after. The love of Christ will light your face, and shine from it into a darkened world that needs the light. And from this holy place He will return with you, not leaving it nor you. You will become His messenger, returning Him unto Himself (T-22.IV.3:6-9).

The two of you must dedicate your lives to giving to others the wonderful light that has been reborn at the center of your relationship. This is "the logical conclusion of your union":

Reason now can lead you and your brother to the logical conclusion of your union. It must extend, as you extended when you joined. It must reach out beyond itself, as you reached out beyond the body, to let yourselves be joined (T-22.IN.4:5-7).

You may have thought that your relationship was just supposed to be this wonderful haven into which the two of you could disappear, spending the rest of your lives sipping tea and watching sunsets. Yet from the beginning, the Holy Spirit had other plans for you.

It will not be for you alone, for therein lay its misery. As its unholiness kept it a thing apart, its holiness will become an offering to everyone (T-18.II.6:8-9).

> You have been called, together with your brother, to the most holy function this world contains. It is the only one that has no limits, and reaches out to every broken fragment of the Sonship with healing and uniting comfort. This is offered you, in your holy relationship....The holy light that brought you together must extend, as you accepted it (T-18.I.13:1-3,6).

This gives us a much greater appreciation for the line we quoted earlier: "You do not understand what you accepted" (T-18.III.4:11). For, from the Holy Spirit's perspective, this was a great deal of the point of the relationship from the very beginning. We tend to think in terms of individual salvation. And so it was a leap to start thinking of two of us being saved together. But two was a lot easier to handle than everyone. Two's company; the whole world's a crowd. Yet the Holy Spirit has no concept of individual salvation. He is absolutely, unequivocally intent on the salvation of everyone, and He knows that it is everyone or no one. And so He is always on the lookout for anyone who will open the door to Him just a crack, so that He can step in and enlist that person in the cause of the Great Awakening. In fact, even before the two of us joined, He was planning to use our relationship for this purpose. The salvation of the world was His goal. And once we did answer Him, just think of the gratitude He had for us.

> He uses everyone who calls on Him as means for the salvation of everyone. And He will waken everyone through you who offered your relationship to Him. If you but recognized His gratitude! Or mine through His! (T-18.II.7:6-9)

Thus, when the two of us joined, a plan was set in motion that would ultimately use our relationship to touch far more people than we would ever have imagined:

> Through your holy relationship, reborn and blessed in every holy instant you do not arrange, thousands will rise to Heaven with you. Can you plan for this? Or could you prepare yourself for such a function? Yet it is possible, because God wills it....It will become the happy dream

through which He can spread joy to thousands on thousands who believe that love is fear, not happiness (T-18.V.3:1-4,5:5).

Yet this is not supposed to be some kind of heroic sacrifice for the sake of the whole. The Course is very clear in saying that only through fulfilling your special function—your part in the salvation of the world—will you find your own salvation (remember our discussion in the last chapter about how you can only be saved through becoming a savior). We are told, therefore, that the Holy Spirit has waiting for each one of us a form of teaching, healing, extending, that is perfectly suited to our special strengths.

And just as each individual has a specially designed function, so does each holy relationship. In fact, our individual special functions, at least in their fullest development, take place within the holy relationship. Our special function is really a joint endeavor: "Neither you nor your brother alone can serve at all. Only in the joint will of you and your brother does healing lie" (T-22.VI.4:5-6).

And just as the individual is saved only by becoming a savior, so the relationship is made fully holy only by extending its light to others. Thus, we will only find the total love between us that we seek when we give our love for each other out to the world. And when we do give that love together, we will find a happiness that we could not have dreamed of.

The extension of the Holy Spirit's purpose from your relationship to others, to bring them gently in, is the way in which He will bring means and goal in line. The peace He lay, deep within you and your brother, will quietly extend to every aspect of your lives, surrounding both of you with glowing happiness and the calm awareness of complete protection. And you will carry its message of love and safety and freedom to everyone who draws nigh unto your temple, where healing waits for him (T-19.IV.1:5-7).

Without this outward extension, the holy relationship is not complete. What was originally invited into the relationship was union, sameness, the overcoming of separation. As long as we are joined with each other but not with others, that union is hemmed in. By extending our joining outward we are really letting the union that was allowed into our relationship to reach its logical conclusion, to spread out and become total. And it is by making that union total that we finally realize our union with totality and with the Creator of totality.

> And now the sameness that you saw [in each other] extends and finally removes all sense of differences, so that the sameness that lies beneath them all becomes apparent. Here is the golden circle where you recognize the Son of God. For what is born into a holy relationship can never end (T-22.IN.4:8-10).

Up until now, what I have been calling the holy relationship may have seemed pretty special: all this attention on one especially significant relationship. Obviously, this relationship is being given a high priority and is eating up attention which we could be giving to other relationships. Yet it is not intrinsically more important than other relationships, nor is it inherently exclusive. For, from the beginning, whether the people involved knew it or not, the relationship was dedicated to the salvation of the world; it was designed to include everyone. And all the attention it has been getting was absolutely necessary if it was ever going to fulfill that function.

The reason for this is obvious. Until you learn how to love each other, you are not ready to go out and save anyone. And so, just as the relationship is practice for Heaven, so it is a classroom in which you learn to give salvation. What you are doing in this very intense classroom is learning all the skills you will need for your larger function together. As the Course says, "And learning this [how to accept healing into your holy relationship], you will have also learned how to release all the Sonship..." (T-17.V.15:2). In other words, in learning to forgive each other, learning to heal each other and love each other, you are in training for giving these same gifts to others. And when you really can forgive each other, there is no one you cannot forgive, no sin, no illusion and no suffering in anyone you cannot overlook:

> When you have looked upon your brother with complete forgiveness, from which no error is excluded and nothing kept hidden, what mistake can there be anywhere you cannot overlook? What form of suffering could block your sight, preventing you from seeing past it? And what

illusion could there be you will not recognize as a mistake; a shadow through which you walk completely undismayed? (T-22.VI.7:1-3)

Remember, when you initially established a common goal, the Christ child was born into your joined hands, "a tiny newcomer, dependent on the holiness of your relationship to let Him live" (T-22.I.8:7). What you have actually been doing since then is raising this Christ child. With each barrier between you that was cleared away, He was "growing up." As everyone knows, raising a child requires enormous focus on the family, not the world. Yet after all this inward attention, at a certain point the child will become an adult, strong enough to go out into the world and fulfill His function. You as parents may not realize this, but this is why He came to you in the first place. He is not content with staying at home, alone with the two of you. He is for the world.

Yet before you can fully unleash this wonderful Spirit onto the world, your relationship must have reached a certain place. Only when you have reached a certain solidity in your union can you more or less graduate from your intense focus on each other and begin to focus primarily on others together. This is not to say that you cannot fulfill a special function together even in the initial period of discomfort. I think that very often that is part of the Spirit's plan for a new holy relationship. It is just that until you get somewhat out of that initial period, what you have to give together is not going to be nearly as full. And if you are not careful, your joint giving may take on the character of empty formality, as opposed to a real extension of the love at the center of your relationship. Also, the busy-ness of it may draw you away from the attention that the relationship needs for its own healing, and focus your attention onto divisive outer issues.

Again, all of this is not to suggest that you should not take on a special function together early in the relationship. I am just suggesting that you not force it. Do it if you are truly led to, and do it gladly. But do not lose sight of your real goal: to embody and extend true, undiluted holiness.

Yet once you do get your own act together, what you can give to the world is incredible. The Course speaks many times of the power of two minds with a shared purpose. Most of us have heard of "the hundredth monkey principle" (although the original "facts" behind it have been discredited), in which the power of an idea suddenly greatly increases when a certain magic number of people (or monkeys) adopt it. The Course's version of this could be called "the second monkey principle." For, from the

Course's standpoint, once just *two* people join they have at their disposal immense power. For they have stepped outside the ego's isolation and so invite to themselves the power of God.

> The world would be completely changed, should any two agree these words ["I want the peace of God"] express the only thing they want.
> Two minds with one intent become so strong that what they will becomes the Will of God. For minds can only join in truth (W-pI.185.2:9,3:1-2).

> It needs but two who would have happiness this day to promise it to all the world. It needs but two to understand that they cannot decide alone, to guarantee the joy they asked for will be wholly shared....It needs but two (T-30.I.17:1-2,4).

> Alone we can do nothing, but together our minds fuse into something whose power is far beyond the power of its separate parts (T-8.V.1:6).

I really think that in the Course's vision of the holy relationship is the germ of a new vision of service and intentional work. A spiritual or charitable or service organization is normally seen largely in terms of form. What words do we say? What programs do we have? What products do we offer? What decisions do we make? What is our vision for our future? How are we doing financially? I think that the Course would say that all of those form issues are effect, not cause. The real content of our work needs to simply be our vision of the Christ in those we serve. We need to see them as guiltless. And, where they are willing, we need to join with them in the common purpose of their salvation and ours.

Yet—and this is the key—we will only be able to really do this if we, the staff of this organization, group or center, are joined in holy relationship. We can only extend real love to the world if we have learned how to see the lovable in each other; if we have learned to release each other from the burden of guilt and care for each other as our own Self. And thus the real question about the functioning of an organization is not, "Are we making the 'right' decision here? Are we working efficiently? Are we cutting costs?" Rather, the question is, "How are we seeing each other?

How are we treating each other?" And then, "How are we seeing those whom we serve? Do we realize that their interests are the same as ours, that their salvation is our own?"

In the early years of the community I am part of our guidance constantly reminded us of this. When you think of a spiritual or intentional community, most minds immediately conjure up romantic images of fertile land covered with gardens, fruit trees, and geodesic domes. And when you think of running a community you immediately think of a group effectively charting its future through sound group decisions, policies and vision. Yet when we approached our guidance, these thoughts of ours were consistently thwarted. Over and over we were told that community was relationships, pure and simple. The only thing we needed to learn was to love each other. And if we did that, the forms and the outcomes would take care of themselves. We initially assumed this meant that we should make the most loving decisions, the ones that would express the most love once implemented. Yet we were told that what really mattered was how loving we were toward each other *while making the decision*. If we fulfilled that condition, then even if we made an impractical decision, the Spirit invited in by our love would somehow correct it.

And, of course, the point of this was that once we had learned to love each other, we would be able to serve the world. In fact, it would be relatively simple, for our service would simply be an extension of the love we had gained for each other.

This vision took us years to really even understand, partly because the guidance came in specific situations, but also because it was just so different from our habitual thinking. And when we tried to implement it, it seemed—and still does seem—so impossible. Yet as time passed and I became more deeply involved in the Course, I realized that our guidance had struck a note that was very similar to the Course's vision of holy relationships. In effect, what we had been told was that *true community is a group holy relationship*.

Because our entire world consists of relationships—because it is in fact simply one big web of relationships—this vision of holy relationships can truly be the basis for a new world. It would be a world in which the spiritual path would be merged with practical living, for in our relationships we would be living our lives and awakening to God in the same act. Think what would happen to our world if we could see relationships in this way, if we could see their foundation as genuine common purpose (instead of individual gratification), if we could see them as invaluable tools for the learning of forgiveness and the transcending of ego, and as mighty conduits for the Spirit to enter and flow out to the world in loving extension. Our concept of marriage, family, friendship, business, service, government, community, city and nation would be completely transformed. Imagine a world joined in the common purpose of transcending the ego and returning to God together! Certainly that is a long way off—I would not even want to guess how long—but the Course says that this future world is actually born right now in each holy relationship.

> The ark of peace is entered two be two, yet the beginning of another world goes with them [just as the beginning of another world was contained in Noah's ark]. Each holy relationship must enter here, to learn its special function in the Holy Spirit's plan, now that it shares His purpose. And as this purpose is fulfilled, a new world rises in which sin can enter not....For the whole new world rests in the hands of every two who enter here to rest (T-20.IV.6:5-7,7:3).

This new world, from the Course's perspective, will be quickly followed by the end of time and its replacement with eternity. Thus, the Course, in one moving passage, calls a holy relationship "a mighty herald of eternity" (T-20.V.1:6), for each one is a harbinger of the end of time:

> Each herald of eternity sings of the end of sin and fear. Each speaks in time of what is far beyond it. Two voices raised together call to the hearts of everyone, to let them beat as one. And in that single heartbeat is the unity of love proclaimed and given welcome (T-20.V.2:1-4).

Thus, says the Course, what began so "harmlessly" with two people seeing a common goal, has ultimately grown into something of unimaginable magnitude. For something was born in that moment of joining that we never could have understood back then. Something entered our lives that set our feet on a new path and changed our directions forever. That something slowly grew up as we struggled to forgive each other and relinquish our separateness in favor of oneness. It blossomed as we were able to consistently see the good and the holy in each other, and then dedicate our lives to extending that same vision to others. Unable to be contained, it reached out through us to encircle the entire globe, and to draw it closer and closer to the Eternal Light in which that globe will be shined away. And finally, it drew us right into that Light, into Heaven, having prepared us for the supreme and final joining: our holy relationship with God. Now, at last, we can know what that something was that was born into our relationship and led us all this way. It was the Christ Himself. Once He was let in, it was all over. The logical and inevitable conclusion of His entry was the ending of the separation.

Index